VOLODYMYR ZELENSKY

IN HIS OWN WORDS

VOLODYMYR ZELENSKY

IN HIS OWN WORDS

EDITED BY

LISA ROGAK AND
DAISY GIBBONS

PEGASUS BOOKS
NEW YORK LONDON

VOLODYMYR ZELENSKY IN HIS OWN WORDS

Pegasus Books, Ltd.
148 West 37th Street, 13th Floor
New York, NY 10018

First Pegasus Books cloth edition October 2022

Interior design by Maria Fernandez

Library of Congress Cataloging-in-Publication Data is available.

ISBN: 978-1-63936-314-8

10 9 8 7 6 5 4 3 2 1

Printed in the United States of America
Distributed by Simon & Schuster
www.pegasusbooks.com

For Alex
—L. R.

To everyone in Ukraine and around
the world who is fighting for their right
to self-determination.
—D. G.

CONTENTS

INTRODUCTION

"You've never seen someone like me."
—Volodymyr Zelensky

Since February 24, 2022, when Russia launched its invasion into Ukraine, people all over the world have reacted with horror and revulsion while also being heartened by the inspirational words and courageous actions of Volodymyr Zelensky, the forty-four-year-old president of Ukraine. Amid unthinkable tragedy and despite great personal risk, Zelensky has remained in the beleaguered capital of Kyiv to support his fellow Ukrainians while standing up to a sociopathic madman who possesses the power to launch World War III. And Zelensky demands that the West do much, much more.

Zelensky is the hero we didn't know we needed . . . or maybe we did. More than a few have called him the Churchill of our time, and since the onset of the Russian invasion, governments around the world have awarded him their highest honors.

This former comedian and actor, elected in 2019 with 73% of the vote, has shown his mettle time and time again. Through his actions and words he's proven that he's an Everyman whose sole motivation is improving the lives of his fellow Ukrainians, unlike his predecessors, overly stuffed oligarchs whose primary intent in getting elected was to stuff their own pockets.

Though Zelensky was elected with no previous experience in government, he hit the ground running from day one, determined to follow in the footsteps of the character he created on his wildly successful *Servant of the People* TV show.

In addition to being the first presidential candidate in Ukraine—or anywhere—to run a campaign almost exclusively through digital and online communication, Zelensky is the first modern president to manage a war and invasion primarily through social media, Zoom interviews, and speeches, enabling citizens all over the world to witness a bravery that has rarely been seen, well, since Churchill.

In a matter of days, Volodymyr Zelensky made an indelible impact on people all over the world, making them feel optimistic about their lives, the world, and democracy. In short, the president of Ukraine has been the one leader able to unify people with strongly differing opinions who haven't been able to agree on anything in a very long time.

The best way for people who are curious to know more about this inspiring man is through his own words. With *Volodymyr Zelensky In His Own Words,* readers can do just that, with his views and thoughts condensed down into bite-sized bits.

Zelensky has won accolades from all corners of the world, inspiring people everywhere to work harder and strive to be better individuals through his example. Anyone looking for inspiration can turn to any page in this book and find enlightenment and motivation, not to mention hope for the human race.

LIST OF QUOTES

THE QUOTES

ON ABORTION

I think that a person chooses an abortion [herself]. I think it should not be banned. Why are we even talking over what we ought to ban? To be honest, we need to meddle with human freedoms less.

—*RBC-Ukraine*, April 18, 2019

ON HIS ACTING SKILLS

What the viewer loves in an actor, this feeling of humanity, of course I use it. And that's very easy to do, because I remain myself.

—*The New Yorker*, November 4, 2019

ON BECOMING A UKRAINIAN CITIZEN

To everyone who is ready to build a new and successful Ukraine, I will happily give you Ukrainian citizenship. You should come to Ukraine as if you are coming home—not visiting as a guest. We are waiting for you. Don't bring souvenirs from abroad, bring us your knowledge, experience, and values. All of this will help us start a new epoch.

—Inaugural address, May 20, 2019

ON BEING ALONE

I can't stand eating alone. And it's difficult to fall asleep when my wife isn't here.

—*Viva*, March 15, 2016

ON BEING CALLED A NAZI

How can I be a Nazi? Explain it to my grandfather, who went through the entire war in the infantry of the Soviet army, and died a colonel in an independent Ukraine.

—The Detroit Jewish News, February 28, 2022

Putin talks about the Ukrainian government as being full of Neo-Nazis. There are rare occasions when I smile and when I laugh, and to me [this is] a joke. I cannot take this statement seriously.

—CNN, March 20, 2022

ON CANADA

Everyone is talking about NATO, but we are not joining
anywhere yet. Canada is full of Ukrainians. Can we
sign some kind of military support agreement with the
Canadians?

—GordonUA.com, December 26, 2018

ON CANCEL CULTURE

I have always been against bans. And I don't like when the policy of prohibitions affects artists. It is nonsense! But as soon as an artist becomes not an artist, but a politician, he immediately ceases to be an artist.

—*Delfi*, July 11, 2017

ON THE CAPITOL RIOTS IN THE U.S.

We are used to believing that the United States has the ideal democratic institutions, where power is transferred calmly. In Ukraine, we lived through two revolutions, we understood such things can happen in the world. But that it could happen in the United States? No one expected that. After this, I believe it would be very difficult for the world to see the United States as a symbol of democracy.

—*Axios on HBO*, January 31, 2021

I think it was a heavy blow to U.S. democracy.

—*Finbalance*, February 1, 2021

ON HIS CHILDHOOD

We lived in Mongolia for almost four years. We learned the Mongolian language, rode Mongolian horses, and walked along the hills, which were dotted with tulips.

—GordonUA.com, December 26, 2018

[As a kid] I dreamed of becoming a border guard, then a translator and then a diplomat.

—GordonUA.com, December 26, 2018

School is where you have your first friendship, first love, first conflicts, all your firsts, where you have that first knowledge that you absorb like a sponge. It was a crazy fun time. I don't like to look back on the past much, but school is the only thing from the past I want to go back to. A river you want to jump in a second time.

—Instagram, September 1, 2017

ON HIS CHILDREN

I feel like I'm on the same wavelength with them, I speak their language. My son and I communicate in an ancient language of gestures and sounds, stand on all fours in front of each other and growl. Children bring me back to the sandbox, where I feel comfortable.

—*Viva*, January 9, 2014

I have incredible love for my children. I hope it's mutual.

—*Gordon Boulevard*, May 15, 2006

It is a great pleasure having children. Stop watching this if you don't have children yet—you know what you could be doing right now!

—Instagram, June 1, 2018

ON CLIMATE CHANGE

We don't have a reserve planet. We live here and just once.

—Speech, September 23, 2020

Further development of mankind depends on what governments and businesses do in this decade. If we fail to reduce the pace of climate change, after 2030 the social and economic losses will be so significant that no one in the world will be able to shut themselves off from this threat within their national borders. No one will be able to beat the climate with political populism.

—UKRInform.net, January 11, 2021

Ukraine's long-term goal is to achieve carbon neutrality, and we will make every effort to minimize the time to achieve this goal. Ukraine also seeks to align its climate policy and legislation with the European Green Deal.

—Speech, December 13, 2020

ON COMPROMISE

Compromises can be made, but they must not be about betraying my country.

—*Bild*, March 11, 2022

ON COOPERATION

"Nothing depends on me" is a myth. Together we can do everything.

—Speech, November 21, 2020

ON CORRUPTION IN GOVERNMENT

This is the first government where there is no corruption [at the top]. But not stealing is not enough.

—Speech, March 4, 2020

People say to me, "Oh, we can't force the people to pick up their dog poop, drive according to the rules, stop drunk driving, it's in our mentality, it's like Moses and forty years in the desert." This all a lie! The problem isn't mentality, the problem is starting with the president. If the leadership allows itself whatever it wants, we look and say okay, we're allowed, too.

—*ICTV*, March 24, 2019

ON COVID-19

COVID-19 has shown that the global world is not just a world without borders. This is also a global responsibility, when not seven, not 20, but at least 193 countries should be involved in counteracting common threats.

—Speech, September 23, 2020

Local authorities want to please voters. They sabotage government decisions and [play] a game of "bad cop" in the capital and "good cop" on the ground. There may be more votes for you in your region, but the number of sick and dead will be your fault.

—Speech, October 20, 2020

The year 2020 really turned our traditional perceptions upside down. The word "negative" brings people joy, happiness, because a negative test means recovery. But the word "positive" on the other hand came to be negative.

—Facebook, November 12, 2020

ON COVID-19 (CONTINUED)

After Chernobyl, authorities gathered people for a May Day demonstration. No one was afraid at the time, because "radiation is invisible." Coronavirus is also invisible, so we ask you to stay home. No one will steal the beaches and no one will take out the sand. The parks will not disappear anywhere. Strolls can wait.

—Speech, April 1, 2020

There is a paradox in this whole situation. Everyone is advised to wear masks, but coronavirus actually takes the masks off people, because someone is ready to help by giving the shirt off his back while someone else is willing to line his pockets from human misery.

—Speech, March 23, 2020

We have all promised ourselves: I will improve my English, sort out the mess on my computer desktop, and this Monday I will definitely do ab exercises. Well, maybe *next* Monday, I will definitely do ab exercises.

—Speech, April 7, 2020

ON CRIMEA

Russia says Ukraine seeks to join NATO [in order] to return Crimea by force. It is gratifying that the words "return Crimea" appear in their rhetoric.

—Speech, February 19, 2022

Occupation of Crimea casts doubts on the effectiveness of the entire international security system. Without restoring the trust in it, not a single state can be sure that it wouldn't become the next victim of occupation.

—*Al-Jazeera*, August 23, 2021

Crimea was the heart of Ukraine: Sunny, kind, bright. Seven years ago, our heart was torn out. We will never forget who did it, and we will never forget who allowed it. [Our] heart must be returned.

—Speech, February 26, 2021

ON CRIMEA (CONTINUED)

Forget that Ukraine will forget about Crimea.

—Speech, March 12, 2021

Crimea will only be happy in Ukraine.

—*Radio Liberty*, August 19, 2021

ON CRITICISM

Criticism is so relevant. Criticism is good.

—*ICTV*, March 24, 2019

[With people who can take criticism], I like their attitude better, they live easier. I don't I am distressed by it I hold it in me, I worry like crazy, I get all these dumb ideas coming into my head.

—*Behind Their Eyes*, 2010

ON HIS DAILY ROUTINE

I sleep little and work a lot.

—*Viva*, January 9, 2014

ON HIS DETERMINATION

Did I think a year ago that changing the country for the better would be so difficult? No.

Would I have changed my mind if I had known about it then? No.

—Speech, October 20, 2020

ON DIETING

Sometimes I eat bread, but before filming I have to say no because I need to improve my diet. I have a very strict diet: I just don't eat. I can go a week without food. Generally, I love eating. And I generally eat a *lot* . . . But when I work, I just don't notice it: someone brings me something and I'm like an omnivore. If someone put a trash bin next to me I'd probably eat it.

—*Behind Their Eyes*, 2010

ON DIFFICULT QUESTIONS

I'm prepared for difficult questions . . . or you can have a nice time and give me easy ones.

—*Ze!President*, March 21, 2019

ON DIPLOMACY

The language of diplomacy today is our greatest, strongest weapon. And all you need is to know how to use it. Or at least have the desire to use it.

—*Interfax*, December 26, 2018

ON DISINFORMATION

Wash your hands more often after contact with known propaganda.

—Instagram, November 3, 2020

[Ukrainian writer Mikhail Bulgakov] said, "Do not read Soviet newspapers before lunch." Let me add to this classic quote: Don't read corrupt media before lunch and don't watch corrupt TV channels unless you want to get a portion of juicy and preselected nonsense for lunch.

—*Ukraine Pravda*, February 5, 2021

ON DRINKING AND DRUGS

I drink wine. I sleep so little that I can't afford strong drinks like whiskey or vodka. But, in principle, I can drink a bottle of vodka.

—GordonUA.com, December 26, 2018

I do like a drink, I won't hide that, but I'm not a heavy drinker, no.

—*Behind Their Eyes*, 2010

Well, I do sniff coffee, because I am addicted to caffeine. But I don't take any drugs.

—*Pravda Ukraine*, April 8, 2019

Talking to people is my energy drink. My number one energy drink is having a routine.

—*Pravda Ukraine*, April 8, 2019

ON DRINKING AND DRUGS (CONTINUED)

The first time I went to Amsterdam, I definitely had to try everything. We ate some cupcakes and laughed out loud on the train. It was a lot of fun. But many people can't stop using drugs, and that's scary. Maybe when I'm in my seventies or eighties I'll try them again, when there is nothing to lose.

—*Elle Ukraine*, March 2, 2016

ON THE END OF THE WORLD

The end of the world won't happen in Ukraine, I can tell you, because the end of the world started in Ukraine five years ago.

—*Studio Kvartal 95 Online*, May 7, 2017

ON ENVY

Everyone would do well to get rid of envy. Learn to
rejoice and respect the successes of others, using them as a
guide for your growth. For that reason, it is very difficult
for me to stay in America for a long time.

—Delfi, July 11, 2017

ON FACING DEATH

You can try to kill me, I am ready for it, since I know that the idea lives in me and will survive me.

—*Tablet*, February 28, 2022

ON FAME

[People] all tell me their long and different stories and it's not always comfortable. It's difficult, because you should always listen to everything someone has to say. I can't refuse anyone, and I can't cut them off and leave quickly. When there are a lot of people like this in your life, you have nothing left of yourself.

—*Pavel Maljutin*, March 11, 2018

I want to [remain] human. I went out in the street in Odesa in red shorts and people were so surprised. How do you want me to be? Do you want me to be Vlad Incognito, to travel to the Maldives as our former president did?

—*Ze!President*, July 17, 2019

ON FAMILY

One of the most courageous acts for any man is [to bear] responsibility for his family.

—Presidential campaign video, January 9, 2019

When I come home at night and the baby's asleep, I come in, very quietly, I look—and once I see her—that's it, I'm relaxed. Or on stage when I'm performing, it's the moment just before the audience starts clapping. God, it's like being in the Maldives. Shame it's only a second.

—*Behind Their Eyes*, 2010

Becoming a father is a great joy. Becoming a parent is a great responsibility. Being a good parent is a big job.

—Instagram, June 20, 2021

ON FAMILY (CONTINUED)

The First Lady was very worried [adjusting to public life] because she is pedantic and takes everything very seriously. But she's great. My daughter got used to it; at first she was very worried. My son is pretty happy, he says he is the president's son. We explained to him that he can't say that to people. So now he says he's the son of "You Know Who."

—*Ze!President*, July 17, 2019

Being a son is a great happiness, great undertaking, and great responsibility at the same time. It is a joy to have a kind, attentive, caring father, protector, and friend. Having an example to follow is my motivation to constantly move forward and work. There is a desire never to upset, nor disappoint [him].

— Instagram, June 20, 2021

As long as [parents] are alive, we're still children; your back is always covered by these people.

—*Breakfast with 1+1*, September 28, 2017

ON HIS FASHION SENSE

There is no time to follow fashion, my wife arranges my wardrobe. She looks for clothes in stores, then I quickly go there, and, if it fits, I make a purchase. As a rule, I don't even know what brands of jackets or sweaters I sport.

—*Unian*, April 24, 2019

ON HIS FAVORITE BOOKS

I like O. Henry, Jerome K. Jerome, and Edgar Allan Poe, Conan Doyle. My wife says don't tell anyone, but I like the romanticism of Jack London, I like to read it with my children. The children are not very interested, but I reread him for myself, for the heroism.

—GordonUA.com December 26, 2018

I can't read anymore; I have no time. When I open a book at home in bed I immediately fall asleep on the first or second page. But audiobooks, they're the bomb because you can work out at the same time!

—*Breakfast with 1+1*, March 7, 2013

I only read fantasy because I don't want to live in the real world anymore.

—Instagram, November 25, 2018

ON HIS FAVORITE FOODS

When you have a busy schedule, shawarma can be the solution. For those in power, I recommend it!

—*The Times of Israel*, March 2, 2022

ON HIS FAVORITE MOVIES

Once Upon a Time in America is a brilliant movie, and *The Godfather*. I cried at *Rain Man* and at [Jack] Nicholson's genius work in *One Flew Over the Cuckoo's Nest* . . . Sometimes we watch *Pulp Fiction*, one of my favorite Tarantino films. I'll say, "Look at that montage!" and my wife will say, "Vova, reread Tolstoy, *War and Peace*. All your plot twists come from there."

—GordonUA.com, December 26, 2018

ON HIS FEARS

I'm not afraid of anything, except for people.

—CNN, March 20, 2022

ON FIGHTING

I'm the kind of guy that if I get into a fight, I usually don't get out of it. I can lose, but get out in the middle . . . No. The white flag is not our flag!

—GordonUA.com, December 26, 2018

We will not give up and we will not lose. We will fight until the end at sea, in the air. We will continue fighting for our land, whatever the cost.

—Speech, March 8, 2022

ON FORGIVENESS

We will not forgive. We will not forget. We will punish everyone who committed atrocities in this war. We will find all the scum shelling our cities, our people, who was shooting the missiles, who was giving orders. You will not have a quiet place on this earth—except for a grave.

—*The Times of Israel*, March 7, 2022

ON BEING FUNNY

I am a clown, and I'm very proud of it.

—Instagram, February 7, 2019

No problem, Charlie Chaplin was considered the greatest ever clown—a genius—and he fought fascism, by the way.

—*At Gordon's*, March 23, 2019

I act in the Russian language, the kids love me in Moscow. They double over with laughter at my sketches.

—*Tablet*, February 28, 2022

ON HIS FUTURE

It's hard to say. [Being funny] just happened to be a profession. If it later turns into something else and God willing, the Ukrainian market grows and we'll be watched all over the whole world . . . Or maybe it will be a completely different life, with my grandchildren. Or maybe something else . . .

—*Stand Up Boys*, June 19, 2016

You never know where you'll be tomorrow.

—*Cinema Escapist*, August 22, 2017

ON THE FUTURE OF UKRAINE

Right now, every Ukrainian has three paths: to live as you are now and go with the current. Path number two: take your things and earn money abroad to send to your loved ones. That's also fine. Then there's a third path: try yourself to change something in Ukraine. That's what I have chosen.

—*Studio Kvartal 95 Online*, December 31, 2018

Our goal is to strengthen our country, no matter how difficult it gets . . . I don't want to be a weak man.

—*Bild*, March 11, 2022

We are building a country without oligarchs, a country for forty million citizens, not for a hundred on the *Forbes* [list].

—*Euronews*, June 22, 2021

Will we be able to move into the future without arguing about the past?

—Speech, January 22, 2020

I care about how my grandchildren will live.

—GordonUA.com, December 26, 2018

ON GENERATIONAL TRAUMA

Every next crippled generation is a path to a new war.

—Speech, September 25, 2019

ON GLOBAL SECURITY

The architecture of world security is fragile and needs to be updated. The rules that the world agreed on decades ago no longer work. This is a cough syrup when you need a coronavirus vaccine.

—Speech, February 19, 2022

ON GOVERNMENT

When the government forgets its promises, it ceases to hear people and sees no need for change.

—Speech, March 4, 2020

I am not ashamed of our government. But I would like to be proud of it.

—Speech, March 4, 2020

ON GREAT BRITAIN

Britain is definitely on our side. It is not performing a balancing act. Britain sees no alternative for the way out of the situation. Britain wants Ukraine to win and Russia to lose.

—*The Economist*, March 27, 2022

In Britain, you can say what you want. They have such humor there, sharp, jarring, varied. I think it's normal and it's fair.

—*Interfax*, December 26, 2018

ON GROUPIES

Every artist has at least one fan in love with him, you can't
get away from this.

—Gordon Boulevard, May 15, 2006

ON GROWING OLDER

It's nice on the one hand [to be told] that your dreams came true, but on the other hand, when someone with a beard tells me it was their "childhood dream" [to meet me] . . .

—*Stand Up Boys*, June 19, 2016

7 A.M. on the clock
43 on my passport
30 in my heart

—Instagram, January 25, 2021

ON GUN CONTROL

I am against gun legalization. The legalization of weapons today in Ukraine, in a country where there is a war, is wrong.

—*RBC-Ukraine*, April 18, 2019

ON HANGING HIS PRESIDENTIAL PHOTO
IN GOVERNMENT OFFICES

Hang your kids' photos instead, and look at them each time you are making a decision.

—*The New Yorker,* November 4, 2019

ON HAVING A PLAN B

What is Plan B, when we live all our lives according to Plan A?

—*Ukraine Pravda*, January 21, 2019

ON HIS HEROES

Michael Jordan is my favorite basketball player. He used to lure his opponent, sometimes by demonstrating pretend weakness or even signs of illness. He had a variety of secret tricks for making his opponent feel relaxed, imposing a false sense of close victory. And then Jordan would change his tactics dramatically and grab victory at the very last minute.

—*Axios*, June 6, 2021

Meeting Pope Francis in the Vatican was a moment of truth, like proof of reality. Pope Francis is doing his best to achieve peace and harmony in different parts of the world and [has] repeatedly prayed for peace in Ukraine. I felt understanding and hope from this.

—Instagram, February 8, 2020

Justin Trudeau inspired me to enter politics.

—Twitter, July 2, 2019

ON HISTORY

History is unfair.

—Inaugural address, May 20, 2019

ON HUMAN NATURE

We do first and we think second.

—Breakfast with 1+1, September 28, 2017

People believe in words only for a stretch of time. Then they start to look for action.

—The Guardian, March 7, 2020

ON HUMOR

You *have* to make jokes. In proper countries—well, I *do* think we have a proper country—in open, European countries, the questions of freedom of speech, humor, and open journalism don't even come up . . . they don't even have bodies to regulate [these things]!

—*Interfax*, December 26, 2018

It is more difficult to survive in the provinces without jokes and laughter.

—*Gordon Boulevard*, May 15, 2006

If we can joke [during wartime], I will. The Russians have thousands of military vehicles, and they are coming and coming and coming. There are some cities . . . where they have tank traffic jams.

—*The Economist*, March 27, 2022

ON HUMOR (CONTINUED)

You should take topics for comedy and parody not just from what itches you, but what [matters] to other people. Humor should be socially understood. Just as dogs should walk among dogs, I [have to] walk among people to feel what people are feeling.

—*Pavel Maljutin*, March 11, 2018

There are no sacred cows, because we are not joking about people, but rather about the deeds that people have done.

—*Delfi*, July 11, 2017

Gag humor—where you slip on a banana or throw cakes, for instance—isn't really popular in post-Soviet territories. Perhaps that's because such humor is borne from places where people aren't preoccupied with survival. In post-Soviet countries, satire has historically been more popular.

—*Cinema Escapist*, August 22, 2017

You need to laugh every day.

—Instagram, April 1, 2017

ON HIS INAUGURATION

Dear deputies! I see you have scheduled the inauguration on a working day, on a Monday. I see a positive in this: it means you are ready to get to work.

—Inaugural address, May 20, 2019

ON INDEPENDENCE

The desire for independence is embedded in our genetic code.

—Speech, August 24, 2019

Our independence must be defended every day and by each of us. For some, this will be done with a weapon in their hands; for others, with a teacher's pointer; for still others with a surgeon's scalpel.

—Speech, August 24, 2020

ON ISRAEL

I respect Israel as hugely special, especially given all the sensitivities around it. It's a united, strong, powerful people. And despite being under the threat of war, they enjoy every day. I've seen it.

—The Times of Israel, January 19, 2020

The Ukrainian and Jewish communities have always been and, I am sure, will be very intertwined, very close. They will always live side by side. And they will feel both joy and pain together.

—The Times of Israel, March 20, 2022

ON JAPANESE CULTURE

For me it was a great honor taking part in the enthrone-
ment of Emperor Naruhito. The execution of an ancient
rite in modern Japan was an example of how deep respect
for traditions and the introduction of the latest technology
to improve everyone's life can coexist in one country.

—Instagram, October 22, 2019

ON BEING JEWISH

[In school], you had to be the star student. If you're better than everyone else, then you could find your place among the best—maybe. It's not like that today.

—*Pavel Maljutin*, March 11, 2018

I have Jewish blood. And I'm president. And nobody cares. Nobody asks me about it.

—*The Times of Israel*, January 19, 2020

The fact that I am a Jew is about the 20th question among my characteristics.

—*The New York Times*, April 24, 2019

You know the old joke about the difference between Jewish moms and rottweilers? Well, rottweilers sometimes let go of you.

—*The Vesti*, March 27, 2019

ON JOURNALISTS

I want to thank all . . . journalists who haven't forgotten their profession and why they were born, which was to show people the truth.

—Facebook, November 24, 2017

ON KEEPING BUSY

You know [Michael] Phelps, the well-known Olympic champion? That's how I see my birthday: The year starts and I dive in and go! [I] swim, swim, swim. [I take a breath on] my birthday, and it starts again. That's how I work, I give everything.

—*Behind Their Eyes*, 2010

I used to run, run, run all the time, I was afraid to miss something. Today I am wiser and running not everywhere and not so fast.

—*Viva*, March 15, 2016

ON HIS LAW DEGREE

There are rumors that I got good grades.

—*Pavel Maljutin*, March 11, 2018

ON LEADERSHIP

Each leader is responsible not only for the fate of his own country, but also for the fate of the whole world. We all need to realize that a strong leader is not the one who, without batting an eyelid, sends thousands of soldiers to death. A strong leader is the one who protects everyone's life.

—Speech, September 25, 2019

You can always see whether people are followers or leaders. And one cannot live without the other. Otherwise, the leader will have no one to lead.

—*Viva*, March 15, 2016

ON LEAVING UKRAINE FOR A BETTER LIFE

Many people in post-Soviet countries leave to go where life is better, safer, education is better, and they pay more. All this is true, but maybe you should calmly realize your disadvantages, believe in yourself, and make your country just as cool.

—*Delfi*, July 11, 2017

I don't want to send money to other countries, so it has to be profitable to live and work in Ukraine.

—*Newsweek*, January 20, 2020

ON LEGALIZING MEDICAL MARIJUANA

I think that this is fine.

—*RBC-Ukraine*, April 18, 2019

ON LEGALIZING PROSTITUTION

Sex for money? Honestly, guys, I think we have the opportunity to set up "Las Vegas" [in Ukraine]. Society would not mind as taxes would be paid. As a result, any abandoned city can be developed.

—*RBC-Ukraine*, April 18, 2019

ON LGTBQ RIGHTS

We all live together in an open society where each person can choose the language they want to speak, their ethnicity, and [sexual] orientation. Leave those people be, for God's sake!

—Press conference, October 10, 2019

ON THE LIMITS OF SOCIAL MEDIA

My most important and sincere words for you are not on social networks, but at home, in the kitchen, alone, openly, face to face, over a drink.

—Instagram, June 20, 2021

ON LOVE

Love is . . . a constant feeling of discomfort when a loved one is not around. And you constantly want to take her hand, talk to her, at least quarrel. This feeling of insatiability is the whole buzz, this is what love is!

—*Viva*, January 16, 2014

ON MAKING IT AS AN ACTOR

The people I have beside me are just like me. They're no less talented; they're just not as lucky.

—*Behind Their Eyes*, 2010

ON MAKING MISTAKES

It is not a disaster to make a mistake. A disaster is to create nothing in your life except sewage.

—Speech, April 10, 2020

You know it's not a problem for me. I said from the start that I'm not after ratings or power. If I can't stop the war, then another person who is able to end this tragic history between our countries should come in.

—BBC, October 12, 2020

ON MANNERS

I don't have time for niceties.

—Behind Their Eyes, 2010

ON HIS MARRIAGE

I make the most important decisions with my wife. Without her, it's like being left without a hand. When my wife is not around, I feel like an invalid.

—GordonUA.com, December 26, 2018

@olenazelenska_official! Thank you for every word and every look. For every step we've taken together. We still have a long way to go . . . with unexpected turns and unforgettable experiences. And I'm happy about that. Because with you, I can do everything in the world.

—Instagram, February 6, 2020

At home, I'm a little useless. I forget birthdays and lose money and mobile phones.

—Gordon Boulevard, May 15, 2006

You know, wives sometimes get offended, they say, "I dreamed you cheated on me." "But it was a dream!" "I don't care."

—*Social Life*, February 26, 2016

ON HIS MARRIAGE (CONTINUED)

Thank God my wife is jealous because it means that she still loves me.

—*Social Life,* February 26, 2016

ON THE MILITARY

There can be no strong army in a place where the authorities do not respect the people who every day sacrifice their lives for the country.

—Inaugural address, May 20, 2019

Only a modern and capable army will guarantee the continued observance of peace and be the key to Ukraine's security.

—Speech, October 20, 2020

The most important thing that our army has is people.

—Speech, October 20, 2020

Positive, light, patriotic people, defending [the country while] respecting each other. If you could only see how these one-and-a-half-thousand lads [treat each other with] such openness at the highest level, while they risk their lives while defending our lives.

—*Breakfast with 1+1*, August 21, 2014

ON THE MILITARY (CONTINUED)

Our musicians wear body armor instead of tuxedos. They sing to the wounded in hospitals. Even to those who cannot hear them, but their music will break through.

—*USA Today*, April 3, 2022

ON HIS MISSION

All my life I tried to do all I could so that Ukrainians laughed. That was my mission. Now I will do all I can so that Ukrainians at least do not cry anymore.

—Inaugural address, May 20, 2019

ON NATIONAL AUTONOMY

We have to protect ourselves, no one will do it for us.

—Speech, March 12, 2021

ON NATO

If Ukraine were part of NATO, there never would have been escalation in Donbas . . . And it's right [to defend Ukraine] because we are now defending Europe.

—*Finbalance*, February 1, 2021

I've said to the U.S., to the E.U., to everyone, if you don't want to lose Ukraine, you must support it. And NATO membership is a very important signal to the Russian Federation.

—BBC, October 12, 2020

If someone says that for us, NATO is a fantasy, I say that the idea of war between Ukraine and Russia was also once a fantasy.

—BBC, October 12, 2020

ON NATO (CONTINUED)

The alliance is afraid of controversial things and confrontation with Russia. I have cooled down regarding this question long ago after we understood that NATO is not prepared to accept Ukraine.

—ABC News, March 8, 2022

I think I express myself like a president on [the E.U.'s] level, or the representative of a country on the same level as theirs . . . It's not fair, this attitude towards Ukraine as some Second [or] Third World country.

—*Telechannel 1+1*, June 24, 2021

ON PARTNERING WITH OTHER NATIONS

We will defend our land with or without the support of partners, whether they give us hundreds of modern weapons or five thousand helmets. We appreciate any help, but everyone should understand that these are not charitable contributions. This is your contribution to the security of Europe and the world.

—Speech, February 19, 2022

ON PATIENCE

Patience [comes] when you just want to do something. That's the whole secret of patience.

—*Viva*, March 15, 2016

ON PAYING HIM RESPECT

If you want to start a conversation with me with a word which starts with "D" and ends in "head," I would like you to [remember] that 73% of Ukrainians voted for this d***head.

—*NASH 20.05*, May 20, 2020

ON PEACE

I believe in [peace with Russia]. If I didn't, I wouldn't have run for president of Ukraine. It's very, very hard. We need help from the whole world. But I do not lose faith.

—BBC, October 12, 2020

[Peace talks] go on for many hours . . . often in circles, with people repeating the same things to each other. Here's what I know: people have come to these meetings intending for nothing to happen.

—*Time*, December 2, 2019

Ukraine wants peace. Europe wants peace. The world says it doesn't want to fight, and Russia says it doesn't want to attack. Someone is lying.

—Speech, February 19, 2022

I would never have sought the presidency without having such a goal.

—*The Times of Israel*, January 19, 2020

ON PEOPLE

All I care about is the people. Not politics. Not ambition.
The people are what matter.

—*The Guardian*, April 2, 2019

ON PERFORMING

I don't like [performing at] corporate events. You want a little something in return, you don't want to hear forks scraping plates.

—Behind Their Eyes, 2010

Honestly, it's all the same to me whether they're an oligarch or not, it's basically the same fee for our work. We get the least money at concerts on tour where the audience buys tickets.

—Behind Their Eyes, 2010

When [we perform for soldiers], it's like they transform from soldiers with machine guns and rifles on their shoulders suddenly into children. So different from the cities where we play to spoiled, normal people . . . They catch every line, every gesture.

—Breakfast with 1+1, August 21, 2014

[Being on tour] is a holiday for me . . . of course, I get tired in concerts, but it's a great high, because for a lot of my work I'm just sitting with paper, writing, editing, the whole time [I'm] at a desk.

—Pavel Maljutin, March 11, 2018

ON HIS PERSONAL PHILOSOPHY

I'm interested in everything new. I have a principle: if you do something, do it thoroughly. Otherwise, why waste your time?

> — Facts.ua, November 24, 2006

Indifference makes you an accomplice.

> —BBC News, February 26, 2022

You can look forever at three things: How a fire burns, how water flows, and how politicians talk about the problems in Ukraine. But the problems will not disappear due to our words. We need to work.

> —Speech, October 20, 2020

A smile is everything.

> —Liga.net, June 5, 2018

Beauty requires sacrifice.

> —Instagram, August 7, 2017

ON HIS PERSONAL PHILOSOPHY (CONTINUED)

If you don't know how to do something this way or that
way, be honest and that's it. You have to be honest, so
that people believe you.

—*The Economist*, March 27, 2022

ON HIS PERSONAL WEALTH

I do not talk about earnings because I am very ashamed.
People are so poor.

—GordonUA.com, December 26, 2018

ON PLAYING A PRESIDENT ON TV VS. REAL LIFE

There are more problems, [and] they're catastrophic. They appear like pimples on an eighteen-year-old kid. You don't know where they will pop up, or when.

—*The Guardian*, March 7, 2020

ON THE POLICE

There's a stereotype that I bribe traffic cops, but it's actually the opposite—they give us a note, I sign it and give it back!

—*Behind Their Eyes*, 2010

ON POLITICS

Politics is like bad cinema—people overact, take it too far. When I speak with politicians, I see this in their facial expressions, their eyes, the way they squint.

—*The New Yorker*, November 4, 2019

I am a living person, and I entered politics as a living person. I do not know much, I have no experience, it's all true. But I am the same person as all citizens of Ukraine, and I want to stay that way.

—*Ukraine Pravda*, April 18, 2019

Traffic jams are a nightmare. Why should people suffer because of politicians?

—*RBC-Ukraine*, April 18, 2019

ON HIS POPULARITY

People identify with me because I'm open. I get hurt, I get angry, I get upset. If I don't know something, I honestly admit it.

—*The Washington Post*, March 9, 2019

I'm not iconic, I think Ukraine is iconic.

—CNN, March 1, 2022

ON POST-SOVIET LIFE

They were difficult, stormy, thorny [years], but they were ours together. The whole country cut coupons.

—*New Yorker*, November 4, 2019

ON HIS PREDECESSOR, PETRO POROSHENKO

I am the result of [his] mistakes and promises.

—*Last Chance*, September 29, 2019

I'm not [his] opponent, I'm [his] deliverance.

—*Last Chance*, September 29, 2019

ON BEING PRESIDENT

It's a very difficult job. I don't want to cry or say "Oh, it's so difficult for me. I never see my children; I don't have any hobbies; I don't have time for sports." It's not everybody God gives a chance to have responsibility, and to do something that can help Ukrainians and make a difference and stop the war. I have this chance and I want to use it.

—*The Globe and Mail*, June 21, 2020

This job is very difficult and has great responsibility; like a surgeon, one false move and lives are in danger.

—*Newsweek*, January 20, 2020

In order for our heroes to stop dying I am ready to do everything. And I am definitely not afraid to make difficult decisions, not afraid to lose my own popularity, my ratings.

—Inaugural address, May 20, 2019

My job is to give a signal so that people know how to act.

—*The Economist*, March 27, 2022

ON BEING PRESIDENT (CONTINUED)

I follow the voice of the people.

> —Speech, October 13, 2019

The president can't change the country on his own, but he can give an example.

> —*The Guardian*, March 7, 2020

You can't get used to this work. It's a very difficult profession: it takes all your energy, time, and sometimes desire. You just turn from a person at the end of the evening into some kind of *organism* that doesn't want to think or do anything. Sometimes it doesn't even understand what its family is talking about. It's exhausting, not only for me but also for my family.

> —*TSN*, November 7, 2019

ON PRESIDENT BIDEN

President Biden assured me that Ukraine would never be left alone against Russian aggression.

—Speech, April 2, 2021

President Biden: you are the leader of your brave nation. I wish you to be the leader of the world. Being the leader of the world means to be the leader of peace.

—ABC News, March 16, 2022

All recent American presidents aim to forge a relationship with Russia, and that is [their] right. I do not want to intervene, but if you ask me, the better scenario would be for the U.S. to make it so that Russia starts aiming to forge the relationship with the United States—and the rest of the world. That would be the victory of the world as I see it.

—*Axios*, June 6, 2021

ON PRESIDENT TRUMP

I read [somewhere] that Trump was pressuring me. That was really offensive. Why? Because I'm the president of Ukraine. Maybe we're smaller than the States, but we are an independent country. We proved it to Russia when we withheld our territory, and we continue to prove it. That's why I wasn't pressured by it, I would never have said something like that.

—*Finbalance*, February 1, 2021

Trump noted that our country had been corrupt in previous years, but I told him that we fight corruption every day so please stop saying that Ukraine is a corrupt country, because it isn't true from now on.

—*The Wall Street Journal*, May 18, 2020

[Am I angry at Trump?] Just a little.

—*Finbalance*, February 1, 2021

ON PRESIDENT TRUMP (CONTINUED)

I love all the questions about the USA and Trump. I didn't do anything illegal, I had phone calls with the president of the United States. As the president of Ukraine, I did what I could to have a good, reliable and strong relationship with one of our strategic partners, the United States of America.

—*The Times of Israel*, January 19, 2020

If you're our strategic partner, then you can't go blocking anything for us. [It's] about fairness, not about a quid pro quo.

—*Time*, December 2, 2019

I really wanted to be world famous, but not for this.

—*The New Yorker*, November 4, 2019

ON HIS PRESIDENTIAL OFFICE

Previous inhabitants felt very at home in these surroundings. [But I feel] horribly uncomfortable.

—*The Guardian*, March 7, 2020

This is no place for a normal person. These walls are filled with the symbolism of the past thirty years, they were the site of what brought our country to the condition it's in.

—*The New Yorker*, November 4, 2019

ON PROSECUTING OLIGARCHS

They own the majority of big businesses—lots of people will lose their jobs.

—*Ze!President*, March 21, 2019

ON PUTIN

He sees Ukraine as a part of his world, but that doesn't correspond with what's happened over the last thirty years. Putin has been [in] a bunker for two decades, getting fed information by his coterie. And Ukraine, while he's been in this bunker, has changed significantly, so the way he sees Ukraine is very different from the Ukraine that actually exists in real life.

—*The Economist*, March 27, 2022

This man does not see. He has eyes, but does not see. Or, if he does look, it's with an icy stare, devoid of all expression.

—*Tablet*, February 28, 2022

He said these words, they were stuck in my soul: "Kiev [Kyiv] is the mother of Russian cities." So I have a question for Russians: "Why are you saying such horrid things about your dear mother on the news?"

—*Studio Kvartal 95 Online*, April 13, 2014

ON PUTIN (CONTINUED)

You realize that I can make even Putin laugh? A hollow
laugh, but a laugh all the same.

—*The Wall Street Journal*, April 8, 2019

ON RELIGION

There are things that we never discuss at the table in my family. Religion is number one. We never discuss things that divide families and society.

—RBC-Ukraine, April 18, 2019

Of course, I believe in God. But I speak with him only in those moments which are personal for me, and important.

—The Times of Israel, January 19, 2020

When my daughter was little, I spoke to God when she slept. She slept, I sat next to her and talked about my problems. I speak with God without intermediaries. I don't go to church, not to the synagogue, not to the mosque.

—GordonUA.com, December 26, 2018

The authorities should not interfere in church affairs, I will defend the independence of the church.

—Interfax, August 8, 2019

ON RELYING ON INTERNATIONAL FINANCIAL AID

We're like an actress from a German adult film [who's ready] to take whatever amount from either end.

—GordonUA.com, September 11, 2016

We ask for economic scraps from our neighbors with market economies. The scheme is awesome, it's been verified by the [Romany], except we don't need guitars, and it's not a pyramid scheme! It's simple: You give us your money, and we won't give it back to you. 100% guarantee.

—GordonUA.com, September 11, 2016

ON REMEMBERING THE HOLOCAUST

The most important thing for each country is to honor the memory of its Holocaust victims.

—*The Times of Israel*, January 19, 2020

The victory over Nazism is a treasure gained through suffering, not another reason to go for barbecues.

—Speech, May 9, 2021

ON RETURNING DONBAS AND CRIMEA

Donbas *is* Ukraine. Peace must prevail there, ceasefire must be completed, and foreign military formations must be withdrawn.

—Speech, October 3, 2019

I don't see any other way but a diplomatic solution to this question. Our greatest value is our people, and they shouldn't have to die or leave, and to avoid this we will do all we can.

—*ICTV*, March 24, 2019

ON REVOLUTION

Revolution is the path to desired change.

—Speech, November 21, 2020

ON ROMANCE

The stories of Romeo and Juliet and Bonnie and Clyde are not examples of an ideal relationship. I may be considered unromantic, but I do not see any charm when heroes die for each other.

—*Viva*, January 16, 2014

ON RUNNING FOR PRESIDENT

[My family is] very afraid for me, because they deeply understand what kind of person I am. They know how sharply, extremely, radically fair I am about everything.

—GordonUA.com, December 26, 2018

Should I be president? Well, let's see, I have legal education and that's a plus. I have no political experience, and that is a huge plus.

—*The Wall Street Journal*, March 28, 2019

If you compare [us] two candidates, I think it's better to have a cat in a bag than a wolf in sheep's clothing.

—*Ukraine Pravda*, April 18, 2019

I did not hide from anyone, this was our strategy. I do not go on talk shows, I respect presenters, experts, and journalists, [but] I cannot go where the [other candidates] are, where they're just dogfighting and doing P.R. and nothing useful.

—*Ukraine Pravda*, April 18, 2019

ON RUNNING FOR PRESIDENT (CONTINUED)

I believe that I can only change the country with you. Join my team! Your gender, religion, education, or the language you speak are not important, the main thing is that you DON'T have political experience.

—Instagram, January 1, 2019

ON RUNNING FOR A SECOND TERM

I think there are many promises and I do not want them to go down in history as promises.

—*Ukraine Pravda*, May 20, 2021

ON RUSSIA

The more this beast eats, the more he wants, more and more.

—ABC News, March 8, 2022

We understand that we have catastrophically complex neighbors.

—*Ze!President*, March 21, 2019

[There] is the sound of a new Iron Curtain, which has come down, and it is cutting Russia off from the civilized world.

—BBC News, February 26, 2022

ON RUSSIAN SOLDIERS

[Russian soldiers] have no idea what they [are] doing. They don't know our streets. They don't know our people. They don't understand our mentality, our aspirations, what kind of people here they have, they know nothing. They are just sent to kill and die.

—CNN, March 1, 2022

The invaders do not even mourn their own casualties. This is something I do not understand. And Russia loses 15,000 of its soldiers in a month! [Putin] is throwing Russian soldiers like logs into a train's furnace.

—*The Economist*, March 27, 2022

I recommend the mothers of Russian soldiers look [at these pictures]. Look at the bastards you've brought up. Murderers, looters, butchers.

—Instagram, March 3, 2022

ON SACRIFICE

I am missing my children growing up because I am spending so much time working for others. This is a big psychological challenge, to accept that I am working for people I don't know personally while I miss out on family life.

—*Newsweek*, January 20, 2020

ON SANCTIONS

Sanctions are important, but they can't give people's lives back.

—*Finbalance*, February 1, 2021

ON SEEING ADELE PERFORM IN LISBON

I felt a little hurt that she hasn't come here to perform, to Kyiv. Obviously it's currently too expensive for our country to bring her here. Her concert's totally unique, nothing, just her and the microphone.

—*Stand Up Boys*, June 19, 2016

ON THE *SERVANT OF THE PEOPLE* TV SHOW

I didn't invent all this [the show], I felt all this, I am really feeling this. It would have been impossible to create it all simply because I am a good actor and because someone wrote it well. We wrote it together, we all lived it together.

—GordonUA.com, December 26, 2018

[The show] touches upon a universal desire: all normal people want to live a better life. As the expression goes, a fish rots from the head down. Therefore, everyone wants decent people at the top. When you have that, everyday life can be more normal, and then you don't have to think about survival on a daily basis. Then you can think of other issues, more global ones—like the environment and so on.

—*Cinema Escapist*, August 22, 2017

ON SPEAKING ENGLISH

I speak English "so-so." I have very good pronunciation, but the question is about *what* I'm pronouncing.

—*ILand TV*, April 19, 2017

You know, you don't need really great English to say hi to Sharon Stone. You just open your mouth, and you forget your ABCs and basic words, but it's nice to say hello and shake her hand.

—*Breakfast with 1+1*, March 7, 2013

ON SPEAKING RUSSIAN VS. UKRAINIAN

How else would Russians understand what cretins we are?

—*Evening Kvartal*, March 10, 2017

People in Donetsk should be allowed to speak whatever language they want. There's an information war going on, saying we're not allowed to speak Russian. [Zelensky switches to Russian.] If the Donetsk people have some special request, for example, filling out documents in Russian—I don't see a big problem.

—*Donetsk News*, July 8, 2019

I know Ukrainian quite well, but I am still translating it in my head.

—*ILand TV*, April 19, 2017

I didn't learn Ukrainian because of the law [on speaking Ukrainian on TV], I did it because it's really nice speaking Ukrainian and so I hired a tutor! Soon I'll be whizzing along!

—*Social Life*, April 15, 2017

ON SPEAKING RUSSIAN VS. UKRAINIAN (CONT.)

Everyone's switching to Ukrainian with greater pleasure. The whole of the next generation is going to speak Ukrainian. My children speak Ukrainian easily, they know Russian, but they're starting to translate from Ukrainian into Russian when they speak to me. We have a state language—sorry, well, we are Ukraine—there's the Russian language, it's there, we don't squeeze it out.

—*Ze!President,* March 21, 2019

Many Russian-speaking Ukrainians have switched to Ukrainian [even though] they don't like it . . . because [Russians] killed their brother or father.

—*House TV,* August 5, 2021

The Ukrainian language is an ornament that gives charm to everything. Ukrainian lullabies are the gentlest. Ukrainian poems are the most romantic. Ukrainian anecdotes are the funniest. Conversations are the frankest. Songs are the most heartfelt. And confessions in love in the Ukrainian language are the most ardent.

—*Ukrainian News,* November 9, 2021

ON SWIMMING

When it's the time of year when its muddy, tense outside, and people are depressed—the pool takes it all away. I recommend it to all.

—Instagram, April 9, 2019

ON TECHNOLOGICAL INNOVATION

A digital country is not only convenient, but [makes] bureaucracy and corruption atypical. Get a building permit or register your business in fifteen minutes without leaving your computer. Young parents can receive services online. No state institution will demand from Ukrainians any certificates, orders, or other papers to obtain public services.

—Speech, October 20, 2020

We are creating digital infrastructure, introducing digital residency, and in general, we [are] keeping ahead of other countries in many areas where digital technologies are introduced.

—UKRInform.com, September 4, 2021

There's our old friend Gutenberg, I'd call him a hairy Steve Jobs. What did he do? He created the printing press. The dude tore his historical period a new one. Nice.

—*iForum 2019*, May 23, 2019

ON TRAVELING INTO SPACE

I want to fly into space. Space is very interesting to me: weightlessness, a feeling of lightness!

—*Elle Ukraine*, March 2, 2016

ON TROLLS

There's lots of information about me on various TV channels and sites. I'm the Kremlin's foot, the hairy hand of the U.S., the tooth of the E.U. . . . Who haven't I been? The oligarchs are behind me, I'm fed by oligarchs . . . It's all so boring. So, we're announcing a competition of the best fakes about Zelensky! Upload your fakes about me. Don't show me any mercy, troll me! #ZeFake! I believe in you guys, you're clever.

—Instagram, January 28, 2019

If you [have time to] insult me, it depends on your profession; either someone is paying you and you're not representing yourself, or you're a slacker . . . you're not a patriot, go and pay your taxes, patriot.

—*At Gordon's*, March 23, 2019

ON TRUST

I don't trust anyone at all.

—*Time*, December 2, 2019

There are no people you can trust except our narrow circle. Everyone lies. Everyone takes bribes. Everyone steals—and with a smile on his face.

—*Ze!President*, July 17, 2019

ON TRUTH

We must not fear the truth, we must admit mistakes. Because on the day we dive into the warm bath of illusions, the whole country will sink.

—Speech, March 4, 2020

ON UKRAINE

We are a young country with a thousand-year history.

—Speech, August 24, 2021

Our land is unique, lovely, unbreakable, incredible, amazing, fabulous, wonderful, beautiful. If it was not for our homeland, humanity might not even know these words. After all, they were invented to describe Ukraine.

—Speech, August 24, 2019

I know Ukraine is changing every day. And frankly, if we did not spend so much time and money on the war in the East, Ukraine would make big leaps forward.

—*Axios on HBO*, January 31, 2021

Ukraine is the heart of Europe, and now I think Europe sees Ukraine is something special for this world. That's why [the] world can't lose this something special.

—CNN, March 1, 2022

ON UKRAINE'S HISTORY WITH RUSSIA

We're like Cain and Abel.

—*Meduza*, July 31, 2021

We have a common history, common victories, and many great people. But the policies of Russia are different. They are aimed not at giving but at taking away.

—*Kyiv Post*, September 3, 2021

ON UKRAINIAN AUTONOMY

Large empires have always used smaller countries for their own interests. In this political chess match, I will not let Ukraine be a pawn.

—*The New Yorker*, November 4, 2019

ON UKRAINIAN SACRIFICE

We are paying the highest price of all of the European countries in this war. Everybody is aware, however—the Baltic States, and Poland—that today it's us, tomorrow it might be them.

—*Axios*, June 6, 2021

ON UKRAINIAN SPIRIT

Ukrainians are not used to giving up.

—Speech, November 21, 2021

Many people look at us and think that it will be impossible to achieve the goals we hope for. But we know that our critics are wrong. The people of our country love democracy and freedom and will not let threats take those things away.

—Stanford.edu, September 9, 2021

Nobody's going to break us. We're strong. We are Ukrainians.

—*The Hill*, March 1, 2022

We Ukrainians are a peaceful nation. But if we remain silent today, we will be gone tomorrow!

—*Deutsche Welle*, February 26, 2022

Ukraine fights back.

—Speech, March 12, 2021

ON UKRAINIAN SPIRIT (CONTINUED)

We are a nation that broke the enemy's plans in a week—plans that have been built for years, treacherously, deliberately, with hatred of our country, of our people, of any people who have heart and freedom.

—Axios, March 3, 2022

[After the war], every square today, no matter what it's called, is going to be called Freedom Square, in every city of our country.

—Axios, March 1, 2022

ON UKRAINIANS LIVING IN RUSSIAN-OCCUPIED TERRITORIES

It is difficult for people there to resist information attacks and remain a Ukrainian in their hearts and souls. It is difficult because people have to survive. I am a father myself. And I understand that it is necessary to feed your children.

—*House TV,* August 5, 2021

These are really our Ukrainians. We broadcast there and say, "You and I live in the same house, although in different rooms." But this is temporary. We are still definitely under the same roof.

—*House TV,* August 5, 2021

ON THE UNITED NATIONS

Today, the United Nations is like a retired superhero who has forgotten what he could do. He considers himself a burden, a weak, frail, useless old man whose life was in vain.

—Speech, September 23, 2021

The UN has become software that has saved the world from critical error. At the same time, we must recognize that the system is increasingly failing, attacked by new bugs and viruses, and countering them is not always effective.

—Speech, September 23, 2020

ON THE UNITED STATES

The United States is our strategic partner, and we are very grateful for the support we get.

—*Newsweek*, January 20, 2020

I would call the relationship between the U.S. and Ukraine a tired relationship. *Tired.* Unfortunately.

—*Current Time*, October 11, 2019

ON VICTORY

It's a victory when the weapons fall silent and people speak up.

—Time, December 2, 2019

We believe in victory. It's impossible to believe in anything else.

—The Economist, March 27, 2022

Victory is being able to save as many lives as possible.

—The Economist, March 27, 2022

ON WAR

What can a person say about the war if coffins aren't arriving in his city? Nothing.

—GordonUA.com, December 26, 2018

In today's world, there is no longer someone else's war. None of you can feel safe when there is a war in Ukraine, when there is a war in Europe.

—Speech, September 25, 2019

Today, the war is here. Tomorrow, it will be in Lithuania, then in Poland, then in Germany. This is serious.

—ABC News, March 8, 2022

We are not the ones who have started this war. But we are the ones who have to finish it.

—Inaugural address, May 20, 2019

ON WAR (CONTINUED)

When a bomb crater appears in a school playground, children have a question: "Has the world forgotten the mistakes of the 20th century?"

—BBC News, February 26, 2022

[Ukrainians] will continue to kill Russians because Russians have killed their children.

—CNN, March 20, 2022

I will never surrender Ukraine!

—Speech, October 3, 2019

ON WATCHING HIMSELF ON TV

I don't like it! I didn't do it right, I'm not talking like that, my voice is hoarse. Why did you sing like that? You can't sing! You didn't hit a single note. I have a lot of complaints about myself, so I rarely watch myself on TV.

—GordonUA.com, December 26, 2018

If we're at home watching something, I always change the channel if something comes up and I'm being shown on TV.

—*Behind Their Eyes*, 2010

ON HIS WEDDING DAY

We drank a little because it was impossible to relax. It was such an incredible adrenaline rush, such an important day. I kept wondering what would happen tomorrow, how my life would change. To be honest, a wedding is like a change of profession.

—*Today*, December 25, 2018

ON WHO HE IS

I don't like to compare myself to others, and I don't like
to be compared.

—Interfax, December 26, 2018

I'm a person who thinks about things. I'm not prepared to
talk to you if I have no time [to think].

—Interfax, December 26, 2018

You've never seen someone like me.

—RBC-Ukraine, April 18, 2019

I am just a common guy from a common family from a
common industrial town in Eastern Ukraine.

—Kyiv Post, September 3, 2021

I'm a total nerd.

—GordonUA.com December 26, 2018

It is impossible to influence me.

—Elle Ukraine, August 19, 2016

ON WOMEN

Our dear mothers, sisters, daughters, and wives: without you, we are just biological entities. With you, we are people and personalities!

—Instagram, March 8, 2021

[With a female president] Ukraine would have every other country around her little finger! The French would be chasing after us, the Germans would be pining after us, Russia would treat us well.

—*Studio Kvartal 95 Online*, May 7, 2017

Me and the boys thought: how awesome would it be if women decided everything in Ukraine? Everything! Imagine, you go into Parliament and there are 450 blondes there—wonderful!

—*Studio Kvartal 95 Online*, May 7, 2017

ON THE YOUNGER GENERATION

Today, an entire generation, born in independent Ukraine, has already formed. For them, this is a normal state of affairs. It can't be different for them. And that's wonderful. Because this generation is our mental foothold for freedom, democracy, and development. They think differently, they think in a modern way, which means that Ukraine will only move forward.

—Speech, August 24, 2019

I love this country and she [my daughter] loves it, but her generation thinks differently about it. Now we have a chance to change something so that our children do not want to leave for somewhere else.

—GordonUA.com, December 26, 2018

ON THE YOUNGER GENERATION (CONTINUED)

There has never been such a [youthful] government. There are pros and cons to this. There is no experience of corruption—this is a big plus. But everyone is criticizing our council, our government, and me personally. I'm used to it, but it's very difficult for our younger government members.

—*TSN*, November 7, 2019

TIMELINE

1978

Volodymyr Oleksandrovych Zelensky is born in Kryvyi Rih in southern Ukraine to Oleksandr Zelensky, a professor and computer scientist, and Rymma Zelenska, an engineer, on January 25. The family speaks Russian at home.

1980

The Zelensky family moves to Erdenet, Mongolia. Young Volodymyr learns to speak Mongolian and to ride Mongolian horses.

1984

They move back to Kryvyi Rih where Volodymyr enters elementary school.

1995

Zelensky graduates from high school. He enrolls at Kryvyi Rih Economic Institute, part of Kyiv National Economic University, where he pursues the study of law and participates in campus theatre groups and productions. He becomes part of an improvisational theatre group called Kvartal 95—Quarter 95—named after the neighborhood where he grew up.

1997

Kvartal 95 competes on KVN, a televised Russian comedy contest, and the group becomes so popular that they are often featured on the show.

2000

Zelensky graduates from law school. He decides not to pursue a legal career and dedicates himself full-time to a career in entertainment. Kvartal 95 continues to appear on KVN and tours throughout Eastern Europe and Russia. In addition to acting, Zelensky writes many of the sketches and songs the group performs.

2003

Zelensky launches his own entertainment production company, Studio Kvartal 95, with the title of artistic director, and begins to produce and write movies and TV shows.

Zelensky marries Olena Kyiashko, a screenwriter, on September 6. She also grew up in Kryvyi Rih, but she and Volodymyr did not know each other until both attended the same university. They dated for eight years before getting married.

2004

A daughter, Oleksandra Zelenska, is born on July 15.

2005

Zelensky stars as d'Artagnan in a musical version of *The Three Musketeers*, which he also wrote.

2006

Zelensky wins first place on *Dancing with the Stars Ukraine*, competing with his partner Olena Shoptenko. Almost 90% of the national TV audience watched the finale, breaking records. He and Shoptenko wore blindfolds during one segment.

2009

Zelensky plays a randy dentist named Igor in *Love in the Big City*, a romantic comedy modeled after the American franchise *Sex and the City*.

2010

Zelensky reprises the role of Igor in *Love in the Big City 2*.

Zelensky joins the board of the Ukrainian TV station Inter and signs up as general producer.

2011

Zelensky continues his career as a lead in romantic comedies *Office Romance, Our Time*.

2012

Zelensky leaves Inter to launch a working relationship with 1+1, a Ukrainian TV network. He continues to write, produce, and star in movies he develops in conjunction with Kvartal 95.

Zelensky plays Napoleon Bonaparte in the movie *Rzhevsky Against Napoleon*, which debuts on January 25, followed by starring in *8 First Dates*, another romantic comedy, which debuts on March 8.

2013

A son, Kyrylo Volodymyrovych Zelensky, is born on January 21.

Zelensky reprises his role as artistic director with Kvartal 25.

2014

Zelensky serves as the dubbed voice of Paddington Bear for the Ukrainian version of the movie *Paddington*.

2015

In October, *Servant of the People* debuts, a half-hour TV show where Zelensky plays Vasily Petrovych Holoborodko, a high school history teacher who gives a candid YouTube rant on the corrupt state of Ukrainian government. The video goes viral, resulting in his unintended victory as president of Ukraine.

2016

Servant of the People 2, a film based on the TV show, is released on December 29.

2017

Zelensky reprises his role as the dubbed voice of the title bear in *Paddington 2*.

The second season of *Servant of the People* begins airing in October.

2018

Zelensky stars in *Me, You, He, She,* a romantic comedy.

Zelensky announces that he will run for president of Ukraine under his Servant of the People party on December 31.

2019

The third season of *Servant of the People* debuts on March 27. With only three episodes in the season, the last episode airs on March 28, three days before the presidential election.

On March 31, 2019, Zelensky wins more than 30 percent of the vote in the first round of the election.

In the second round on April 21, Zelensky is elected president of Ukraine with over 73 percent of the vote.

On May 20, Zelensky is sworn in as the sixth president of Ukraine. He gives his inaugural address in both Russian and Ukrainian.

The president travels to Brussels on June 4 for a meeting with members of NATO and the European Union.

Zelensky meets with U.S. president Donald Trump on September 25.

Zelensky meets with Russian Federation president Vladimir Putin for the first time on December 9.

2020

Zelensky endorses numerous programs to fight corruption throughout the government and is met with backlash from officials, legislators, and the public. In March, his approval rating stands at 23%.

2021

Zelensky travels to the United States to meet with U.S. president Joe Biden on September 1.

In a nationwide poll conducted in the fall, only 25% of Ukrainians say they support his initiatives.

2022

On February 24, Russia invades Ukraine. Zelensky's bravery and support for his country and her people have yielded countless comparisons to Winston Churchill. He has received awards for bravery from Poland, Latvia, Lithuania, and the Ronald Reagan Freedom Award from the United States. Shortly after the war began, 91% of Ukrainians said they approved of the job he was doing.

In early April, Russian troops began to withdraw from regions around Kyiv.

SOURCES

p. 3   On Abortion: Vladislav Krasinsky and Sergey Shcherbina,
        "Volodymyr Zelensky: It Is Beneficial for Us to Dissolve
        the Rada." *RBC-Ukraine*, April 18, 2019. https://www
        .rbc.ua/rus/news/vladimir-zelenskiy-nam-vygodno
        -raspustit-1555546435.html

p. 4   On His Acting Skills: Joshua Yaffa, "Ukraine's Unlikely
        President, Promising a New Style of Politics, Gets a Taste
        of Trump's Swamp." *The New Yorker*, November 4, 2019.
        https://www.newyorker.com/magazine/2019/11/04
        /how-trumps-emissaries-put-pressure-on-ukraines-new
        -president

p. 5   On Becoming a Ukrainian Citizen: Inaugural Address,
        May 20, 2019. https://www.president.gov.ua/en/news
        /inavguracijna-promova-prezidenta-ukrayini-volodimira
        -zelensk-55489

p. 6   On Being Alone: "Vladimir Zelensky Spoke About Life
        with His Wife and Grown-up Son." *Viva*, March 15, 2016.
        https://viva.ua/lifestar/interesting-conversation/36100
        -vladimir-zelenskiy-rasskazal-o-jizni-s-suprugoy-i
        -povzroslevshem-sine.html

p. 7   On Being Called a Nazi: "Volodymyr Zelensky Was a
        Jewish Comedian. Now the World's Eyes Are on Him."
        Detroit Jewish News, February 28, 2022. https
        ://thejewishnews.com/2022/02/28/volodymyr-zelensky
        -was-a-jewish-comedian-now-the-worlds-eyes-are-on-him/

159

p. 7   On Being Called a Nazi: Fareed Zakaria, "Interview with Ukraine's President Volodymyr Zelensky." CNN, March 20, 2022. https://transcripts.cnn.com/show/fzgps/date/2022-03-20/segment/01

p. 8   On Canada: Dmitry Gordon, "Zelensky: If I Am Elected President, First They Will Sling Mud at Me, Then They Will Respect Me, and Then They Will Cry When I Leave." *GordonUA.com*, December 26, 2018. https://gordonua.com/publications/zelenskiy-esli-menya-vyberut-prezidentom-snachala-budut-oblivat-gryazyu-zatem-uvazhat-a-potom-plakat-kogda-uydu-609294.html

p. 9   On Cancel Culture: Christina Khudenko, "Volodymyr Zelensky about Ukrainianness, Laughter During the War, and Artists in Politics." *Delfi*, July 11, 2017 https://rus.delfi.lv/showtime/news/stars/news/krivorizhanin-vladimir-zelenskij-pro-ukrainskost-smeh-vo-vremya-vojny-i-artistov-v-politike.d?id=49033821&all=true

p. 10   On the Capitol Riots in the US: Jonathan Swan, "Exclusive: Ukraine's Zelensky Calls Riots 'Strong Blow' to U.S. Democracy." *Axios on HBO*, January 31, 2021. https://www.axios.com/ukraine-zelensky-capitol-riots-axios-hbo-f223c6d4-1aee-4779-a26d-f5f0eefb90f2.html

p. 10   On the Capitol Riots in the US: "Zelensky: 'I Have a Simple Question for Biden—Why Is Ukraine Still Not Part of NATO?'" *Finbalance*, February 1, 2021. https://finbalance.com.ua/news/zelenskiy-v-mene--proste-pitannya-do-baydena---chomu-ukrana-dosi-ne-v-nato

p. 11   On His Childhood: Dmitry Gordon, "Zelensky: If I Am Elected President, First They Will Sling Mud at Me, Then They Will Respect Me, and Then They Will Cry When I Leave." *GordonUA.com*, December 26, 2018. https://gordonua.com/publications/zelenskiy-esli-menya-vyberut-prezidentom-snachala-budut-oblivat-gryazyu-zatem-uvazhat-a-potom-plakat-kogda-uydu-609294.html

p. 11   On His Childhood: Dmitry Gordon, "Zelensky: If I Am Elected President, First They Will Sling Mud at Me, Then They Will Respect Me, and Then They Will Cry When I

Leave." *GordonUA.com*, December 26, 2018. https
://gordonua.com/publications/zelenskiy-esli-menya
-vyberut-prezidentom-snachala-budut-oblivat-gryazyu
-zatem-uvazhat-a-potom-plakat-kogda-uydu-609294.html

p. 11   On His Childhood: zelenskiy_official, Instagram, September 1,
2017. https://www.instagram.com/p/BYffW3qnoTD/

p. 12   On His Children: "Vladimir Zelensky About His Beloved
Wife and Children: Exclusive Interview with *Viva!*" *Viva*,
January 9, 2014. https://viva.ua/lifestar/interesting
-conversation/25009-vladimir-zelenskiy-o-lyubimoy-jene-i
-detyah-eksklyuzivnoe-intervjyu-viva.html

p. 12   On His Children: Olga Kungurtseva & Vsevolod
Tsymbal, "Kaveenshchik and TV Presenter Vladimir
Zelensky: There Are No Friends in KVN." *Gordon
Boulevard*, May 15, 2006. http://bulvar.com.ua/gazeta
/archive/s20_3722/2225.html

p. 12   On His Children: zelenskiy_official, Instagram, June 1,
2018. https://www.instagram.com/p/BjeJEgUngVW/

p. 13   On Climate Change: Speech to the United Nations,
September 23, 2020. https://www.president.gov.ua/en
/news/vistup-prezidenta-ukrayini-volodimira-zelenskogo
-na-zagalnih-63889

p. 13   On Climate Change: "Forests, Green Energy, and Ukraine."
UKRInform.net, January 11, 2021. https://www.ukrinform
.net/rubric-polytics/3342618-forests-green-energy-and
-ukraine-zelensky-pens-oped-on-climate-change.html

p. 13   On Climate Change: Speech, International Climate
Ambition Summit, December 13, 2020. https://www
.president.gov.ua/en/news/ukrayina-posilit-svoyu-uchast
-u-globalnij-borotbi-zi-zminoyu-65569

p. 14   On Compromise. Paul Ronzheimer, *Bild*, March 11,
2022. https://www.ukrinform.net/rubric-ato/3426535
-volodymyr-zelensky-president-of-ukraine-you-can
-compromise-but-an-interview-with-bild.html

p. 15   On Cooperation: Speech, November 21, 2020. https
://www.president.gov.ua/en/news/zvernennya-prezidenta
-ukrayini-z-nagodi-dnya-gidnosti-ta-svo-65169

p. 16   On Corruption in Government: Speech, March 4, 2020.
         https://www.president.gov.ua/en/news/vistup-prezidenta
         -ukrayini-volodimira-zelenskogo-na-pozacher-60017

p. 16   On Corruption in Government: "Zelensky with His Wife
         on TV," *ICTV,* March 24, 2019. https://web.archive.org
         /web/20190410094553/https:/www.youtube.com/watch
         ?v=jzkmi1uKfQg

p. 17   On COVID-19: Speech to the United Nations, September 23,
         2020. https://www.president.gov.ua/en/news/vistup
         -prezidenta-ukrayini-volodimira-zelenskogo-na-zagalnih
         -63889

p. 17   On COVID-19: Speech, October 20, 2020. https://www
         .president.gov.ua/en/news/poslannya-prezidenta-ukrayini
         -volodimira-zelenskogo-do-verho-64717

p. 17   On COVID-19: "Video Address of Volodymyr Zelensky
         on the Third Day of Self-Isolation." Office of the
         President, Facebook, November 12, 2020. https://www
         .facebook.com/watch/?v=692063328181188&t=26

p. 18   On COVID-19: Speech, April 1, 2020. https://www
         .president.gov.ua/en/news/zabezpechennya-zasobami
         -zahistu-vid-koronavirusu-socialna-pi-60445

p. 18   On COVID-19: Speech, March 23, 2020. https://www
         .president.gov.ua/en/news/zvernennya-prezidenta
         -ukrayini-shodo-zabezpechennya-zasobami-60261

p. 18   On COVID-19: Speech, April 7, 2020. https://www
         .president.gov.ua/en/news/zvernennya-prezidenta-shodo
         -zahodiv-yakih-vzhivaye-derzhava-60525

p. 19   On Crimea: Speech, February 19, 2022. https://www
         .president.gov.ua/en/news/vistup-prezidenta-ukrayini-na
         -58-j-myunhenskij-konferenciyi-72997

p. 19   On Crimea: "Ukraine's President Pledges to 'Return'
         Russia-annexed Crimea." *Al-Jazeera,* August 23, 2021.
         https://www.aljazeera.com/news/2021/8/23/ukraines
         -president-pledges-to-return-russia-annexed-crimea

p. 19   On Crimea: Speech, February 26, 2021. https://www
         .president.gov.ua/en/news/zvernennya-prezidenta
         -ukrayini-z-nagodi-dnya-sprotivu-okupac-66821

p. 20   On Crimea: Speech, March 12, 2021. https://www
         .president.gov.ua/en/news/zvernennya-prezidenta
         -ukrayini-shodo-ostannih-rishen-rnbo-67109

p. 20   On Crimea: Volodymyr Zelensky. *Radio Liberty*, August 19,
         2021. https://www.youtube.com/watch?v=8-O2r_RrvWE

p. 21   On Criticism: "Zelensky with His Wife on TV," *ICTV*,
         March 24, 2019. https://web.archive.org/web
         /20190410094553/https:/www.youtube.com/watch?v
         =jzkmi1uKfQg

p. 21   On Criticism: "Behind the Eyes of Vladimir Zelensky."
         Behind Their Eyes, 2010. https://www.youtube.com
         /watch?v=1W2fTpGNIFY

p. 22   On His Daily Routine: "Vladimir Zelensky About His
         Beloved Wife and Children: Exclusive Interview with
         Viva!" *Viva*, January 9, 2014. https://viva.ua/lifestar
         /interesting-conversation/25009-vladimir-zelenskiy-o
         -lyubimoy-jene-i-detyah-eksklyuzivnoe-intervjyu-viva.html

p. 23   On His Determination: Speech, October 20, 2020. https
         ://www.president.gov.ua/en/news/poslannya-prezidenta
         -ukrayini-volodimira-zelenskogo-do-verho-64717

p. 24   On Dieting: "Behind the Eyes of Vladimir Zelensky."
         Behind Their Eyes, 2010. https://www.youtube.com
         /watch?v=1W2fTpGNIFY

p. 25   On Difficult Questions: "Interview with Vladimir
         Zelensky." *Ze!President*, March 21, 2019. https://www
         .youtube.com/watch?v=Ls0tv5M6fMs

p. 26   On Diplomacy: "Zelensky: The Servant of the People
         Party is Going into Politics." *Interfax*, December 26, 2018.
         https://web.archive.org/web/20190103055829/https
         ://ua.interfax.com.ua/news/election2019/555634.html

p. 27   On Disinformation: zelenskiy_official, Instagram,
         November 3, 2020. https://www.instagram.com/p
         /CHHrAQ9h313/

p. 27   On Disinformation: Valentina Romanenko, "Zelensky
         Paraphrased Bulgakov: 'Don't Read Corrupt Media before
         Dinner.'" *Ukraine Pravda*, February 5, 2021. https://www
         .pravda.com.ua/rus/news/2021/02/5/7282484/

p. 28   On Drinking and Drugs: Dmitry Gordon, "Zelensky: If
         I Am Elected President, First They Will Sling Mud at
         Me, Then They Will Respect Me, and Then They Will
         Cry When I Leave." *GordonUA.com*, December 26, 2018.
         https://gordonua.com/publications/zelenskiy-esli-menya
         -vyberut-prezidentom-snachala-budut-oblivat-gryazyu
         -zatem-uvazhat-a-potom-plakat-kogda-uydu-609294.html

p. 28   On Drinking and Drugs: "Behind the Eyes of Vladimir
         Zelensky." *Behind Their Eyes*, 2010. https://www.youtube
         .com/watch?v=1W2fTpGNIFY

p. 28   On Drinking and Drugs: "Coffee and Wine. I Don't Use
         Drugs." *Pravda Ukraine*, April 8, 2019. https://www
         .youtube.com/watch?v=WNRUDEyxh_0

p. 28   On Drinking and Drugs: "Coffee and Wine. I Don't Use
         Drugs." *Pravda Ukraine*, April 8, 2019. https://www
         .youtube.com/watch?v=WNRUDEyxh_0

p. 29   On Drinking and Drugs: MS Rybik, "Interview: Vera
         Brezhneva and Vladimir Zelensky." *Elle Ukraine*,
         March 2, 2016. https://elle.ua/ludi/interview/intervyu
         -vera-brejneva-i-vladimir-zelenskiy/

p. 30   On the End of the World: "Putin is a Little Boy Who
         Can Control His Gas: The Best Monologues of Zelensky."
         Studio Kvartal 95 Online, May 7, 2017. https://www
         .youtube.com/watch?v=h_6l8Na_KNE

p. 31   On Envy: Christina Khudenko, "Volodymyr Zelensky about
         Ukrainianness, Laughter During the War, and Artists in
         Politics." *Delfi*, July 11, 2017. https://rus.delfi.lv/showtime
         /news/stars/news/krivorizhanin-vladimir-zelenskij-pro
         -ukrainskost-smeh-vo-vremya-vojny-i-artistov-v-politike.d
         ?id=49033821&all=true

p. 32   On Facing Death: Bernard-Henri Levy, "Ukraine's Hero
         President Z." *Tablet*, February 28, 2022. https://www
         .tabletmag.com/sections/israel-middle-east/articles
         /ukraines-hero-president-z

p. 33   On Fame: "Interview Vladimir Zelensky: 'As Soon As I Plan on
         Going into Politics, I'll Tell You.'" *Pavel Maljutin*, March 11,
         2018. https://www.youtube.com/watch?v=1tcBoqj2yEI

p. 33   On Fame: "They Steal with a Smile!" *Ze!President*, July 17,
          2019. https://www.youtube.com/watch?v=hKJ7gOZ70CU
p. 34   On Family: Presidential Campaign video, January 9, 2019.
          https://www.youtube.com/watch?v=kX0kFXBt0oU
p. 34   On Family: "Behind the Eyes of Vladimir Zelensky."
          Behind Their Eyes, 2010. https://www.youtube.com
          /watch?v=1W2fTpGNIFY
p. 34   On Family: zelenskiy_official, Instagram, June 20, 2021.
          https://www.instagram.com/p/CQV5aedhxc3/
p. 35   On Family: "They Steal with a Smile!" *Ze!President*, July 17,
          2019. https://www.youtube.com/watch?v=hKJ7gOZ70CU
p. 35   On Family: zelenskiy_official, Instagram, June 20, 2021.
          https://www.instagram.com/p/CQV5aedhxe3/
p. 35   On Family: "Volodymyr Zelensky Talked About His
          Relationship with his Parents." *Breakfast with 1+1*,
          September 28, 2017. https://www.youtube.com/watch?v
          =FtZKI11bgXo
p. 36   On His Fashion Sense: "Ukraine's Next First Lady: Main
          Facts about Olena Zelenska." *Unian*, April 24, 2019.
          https://www.unian.info/politics/10529706-ukraine-s
          -next-first-lady-main-facts-about-olena-zelenska.html
p. 37   On His Favorite Books: Dmitry Gordon, "Zelensky: If I
          Am Elected President, First They Will Sling Mud at Me,
          Then They Will Respect Me, and Then They Will Cry
          When I Leave." GordonUA.com December 26, 2018.
          https://gordonua.com/publications/zelensky-esli-menya
          -vyberut-prezidentom-snachala-budut-oblivat-gryazyu
          -zatem-uvazhat-a-potom-plakat-kogda-uydu-609294.html
p. 37   On His Favorite Books: "Volydymyr Zelenskyi." *Breakfast
          with 1+1*, March 7, 2013. https://www.youtube.com
          /watch?v=fnS_RPhG7Vc
p. 37   On His Favorite Books: zelenskiy_official, Instagram,
          November 25, 2018. https://www.instagram.com/p
          /BqmJJ3FBbj0/
p. 38   On His Favorite Foods: Philissa Cramer, "18 Things to
          Know about Jewish Defender of Ukrainian Democracy
          Volodymyr Zelensky." *The Times of Israel*, March 2, 2022.

https://www.timesofisrael.com/18-things-to-know-about
-jewish-defender-of-ukrainian-democracy-volodymyr
-zelensky/

p. 39   On His Favorite Movies: Dmitry Gordon, "Zelensky: If
          I Am Elected President, First They Will Sling Mud at
          Me, Then They Will Respect Me, and Then They Will
          Cry When I Leave." *GordonUA.com*, December 26, 2018.
          https://gordonua.com/publications/zelenskiy-esli-menya
          -vyberut-prezidentom-snachala-budut-oblivat-gryazyu
          -zatem-uvazhat-a-potom-plakat-kogda-uydu-609294.html

p. 40   On His Fears: CNN, March 20, 2022. https://www.cnn
          .com/2022/03/20/politics/zelensky-putin-ukraine
          -negotiations-war-cnntv/index.html

p. 41   On Fighting: Dmitry Gordon, "Zelensky: If I Am Elected
          President, First They Will Sling Mud at Me, Then They
          Will Respect Me, and Then They Will Cry When I
          Leave." *GordonUA.com* December 26, 2018. http
          s://gordonua.com/publications/zelenskiy-esli-menya
          -vyberut-prezidentom-snachala-budut-oblivat-gryazyu
          -zatem-uvazhat-a-potom-plakat-kogda-uydu-609294.html

p. 41   On Fighting: Speech to British House of Commons,
          March 8, 2022. https://www.cnn.com/europe/live-news
          /ukraine-russia-putin-news-03-08-22/h_941c2184925
          ffb2ecc79546e6c286a25

p. 42   On Forgiveness: "Zelensky Says 'We Will Not Forgive'
          after Russians Kill Fleeing Civilians." *The Times of Israel*,
          March 7, 2022. https://www.timesofisrael.com/liveblog
          _entry/zelensky-says-we-will-not-forgive-after-russians
          -kill-fleeing-civilians/

p. 43   On Being Funny: zelenskiy_official, Instagram, February 7,
          2019. https://www.instagram.com/p/Btk0UmPI1re/

p. 43   On Being Funny: "Zelensky: Me, A Clown? No Problem."
          At Gordon's, March 23, 2019. https://www.youtube.com
          /watch?v=I5yKqKsXWbc

p. 43   On Being Funny: Bernard-Henri Levy, "Ukraine's Hero
          President Z." *Tablet*, February 28, 2022. https://www

.tabletmag.com/sections/israel-middle-east/articles
/ukraines-hero-president-z

p. 44   On His Future: "Star Interview: Volodymyr Zelenskyi."
Stand Up Boys, June 19, 2016. https://www.youtube.com
/watch?v=dkf8OK7TkLc

p. 44   On His Future: Anthony Kao, "Interview: Vladimir
Zelenskiy on Playing Ukraine's President in *Servant of the
People*." *Cinema Escapist*, August 22, 2017. https://www
.cinemaescapist.com/2017/08/interview-vladimir-zelenskiy
-playing-ukraines-president-servant-people/

p. 45   On the Future of Ukraine: Volodymyr Zelensky, "I Am
Running for President of Ukraine." *Studio Kvartal 95
Online*, December 31, 2018. https://www.youtube.com
/watch?v=Jjc4kcx8mlw

p. 45   On the Future of Ukraine: Paul Ronzheimer, *Bild*, March 11,
2022. https://www.ukrinform.net/rubric-ato/3426535
-volodymyr-zelensky-president-of-ukraine-you-can
-compromise-but-an-interview-with-bild.html

p. 45   On the Future of Ukraine: "Ukraine's Volodymyr
Zelensky Speeds Up Corruption Crackdown, One
Oligarch at a Time." *Euronews*, June 22, 2021. https
://www.euronews.com/my-europe/2021/06/22/ukraine
-s-volodymyr-zelensky-speeds-up-corruption-crackdown
-one-oligarch-at-a-time

p. 45   On the Future of Ukraine: Speech, January 22, 2020.
https://www.president.gov.ua/en/news/zvernennya
-prezidenta-z-nagodi-dnya-sobornosti-ukrayini-59353

p. 45   On the Future of Ukraine: Dmitry Gordon, "Zelensky:
If I Am Elected President, First They Will Sling Mud at
Me, Then They Will Respect Me, and Then They Will
Cry When I Leave." *GordonUA.com*, December 26, 2018.
https://gordonua.com/publications/zelenskiy-esli-menya-
vyberut-prezidentom-snachala-budut-oblivat-gryazyu-
zatem-uvazhat-a-potom-plakat-kogda-uydu-609294.html

p. 46   On Generational Trauma: Speech to the United Nations,
September 25, 2019. https://www.president.gov.ua/en

/news/vistup-prezidenta-ukrayini-volodimira-zelenskogo
-na-zagalnih-57477.

p. 47   On Global Security: Speech, February 19, 2022. https
         ://www.president.gov.ua/en/news/vistup-prezidenta
         -ukrayini-na-58-j-myunhenskij-konferenciyi-72997

p. 48   On Government: Speech, March 4, 2020. https://www
         .president.gov.ua/en/news/vistup-prezidenta-ukrayini
         -volodimira-zelenskogo-na-pozacher-60017

p. 48   On Government: Speech, March 4, 2020. https://www
         .president.gov.ua/en/news/vistup-prezidenta-ukrayini
         -volodimira-zelenskogo-na-pozacher-60017

p. 49   On Great Britain: "Volodymyr Zelensky in His Own
         Words." *The Economist*, March 27, 2022. https://www
         .economist.com/europe/2022/03/27/volodymyr-zelensky
         -in-his-own-words

p. 49   On Great Britain: "Zelensky: The Servant of the People
         Party is Going into Politics." *Interfax*, December 26, 2018.
         https://web.archive.org/web/20190103055829/https
         :/ua.interfax.com.ua/news/election2019/555634.html

p. 50   On Groupies: Olga Kungurtseva & Vsevolod Tsymbal,
         "Kaveenshchik and TV Presenter Vladimir Zelensky:
         There Are No Friends in KVN." *Gordon Boulevard*,
         May 15, 2006. http://bulvar.com.ua/gazeta/archive/s20
         _3722/2225.html

p. 51   On Growing Older: "Star Interview: Volodymyr
         Zelenskyi." *Stand Up Boys*, June 19, 2016. https://www
         .youtube.com/watch?v=dkf8OK7TkLc

p. 51   On Growing Older: zelenskiy_official, Instagram, January 25,
         2021. https://www.instagram.com/p/CKdZJAfhAoI/

p. 52   On Gun Control: "Vladislav Krasinsky, Sergey Shcerbina,
         "Volodymyr Zelensky: It Is Beneficial For Us to Dissolve
         the Rada." *RBC-Ukraine*, April 18, 2019. https://www
         .rbc.ua/rus/news/vladimir-zelenskiy-nam-vygodno
         -raspustit-1555546435.html

p. 53   On Hanging His Presidential Photo in Government
         Offices: Joshua Yaffa, "Ukraine's Unlikely President,
         Promising a New Style of Politics, Gets a Taste of Trump's

Swamp." *The New Yorker*, November 4, 2019. https://www
.newyorker.com/magazine/2019/11/04/how-trumps
-emissaries-put-pressure-on-ukraines-new-president

p. 54   On Having a Plan B: "Zelensky: April 1 Is an Awesome
        Day for Comedian's Victory." *Ukraine Pravda*, January 21,
        2019. https://www.pravda.com.ua/articles/2019/01/21
        /7204341/

p. 55   On His Heroes: David Lawler, Zelensky Interview
        Transcript. *Axios*, June 6, 2021. https://www.documentcloud
        .org/documents/20798133-zelensky-interview-transcript

p. 55   On His Heroes: zelenskiy_official, Instagram, February 8,
        2020. https://www.instagram.com/p/B8UNR1Nlzm2/

p. 55   On His Heroes: @ZelenskyUa, Twitter, July 2, 2019. https
        ://twitter.com/ZelenskyUa/status/1146121659117686787

p. 56   On History: Inaugural Address, May 20, 2019. https
        ://www.president.gov.ua/en/news/inavguracijna-promova
        -prezidenta-ukrayini-volodimira-zelensk-55489

p. 57   On Human Nature: "Volodymyr Zelensky Talked about
        His Relationship with his Parents." *Breakfast with 1+1*,
        September 28, 2017. https://www.youtube.com/watch?v
        =FtZKI11bgXo

p. 57   On Human Nature: Shaun Walker & Andrew Roth,
        "Volodymyr Zelensky: 'My White House Invitation?
        I Was Told It's Being Prepared.'" *The Guardian*, March 7,
        2020. https://www.theguardian.com/world/2020/mar/07
        /volodymyr-zelenskiy-tv-comic-who-became-ukraine
        -president-trump-putin

p. 58   On Humor: "Zelensky: The Servant of the People Party is
        Going into Politics." *Interfax*, December 26, 2018. https
        ://web.archive.org/web/20190103055829/https:/ua.inter
        fax.com.ua/news/election2019/555634.html

p. 58   On Humor: Olga Kungurtseva & Vsevolod Tsymbal,
        "Kaveenshchik and TV Presenter Vladimir Zelensky: There
        Are No Friends in KVN." *Gordon Boulevard*, May 15, 2006.
        http://bulvar.com.ua/gazeta/archive/s20_3722/2225.html

p. 58   On Humor: "Volodymyr Zelensky in His Own Words."
        The Economist, March 27, 2022. https://www.economist

.com/europe/2022/03/27/volodymyr-zelensky-in-his-own
-words

p. 59   On Humor: "Interview Vladimir Zelensky: 'As Soon As I
         Plan on Going into Politics, I'll Tell You.'" *Pavel Maljutin*,
         March 11, 2018. https://www.youtube.com/watch?v
         =1tcBoqj2yEI

p. 59   On Humor: Christina Khudenko, "Volodymyr Zelensky
         about Ukrainianness, Laughter During the War, and Artists
         in Politics." *Delfi*, July 11, 2017. https://rus.delfi.lv/showtime
         /news/stars/news/krivorizhanin-vladimir-zelenskij-pro
         -ukrainskost-smeh-vo-vremya-vojny-i-artistov-v-politike
         .d?id=49033821&all=true

p. 59   On Humor: Anthony Kao, "Interview: Vladimir
         Zelenskiy on Playing Ukraine's President in *Servant of the
         People*." *Cinema Escapist*, August 22, 2017. https://www
         .cinemaescapist.com/2017/08/interview-vladimir
         -zelenskiy-playing-ukraines-president-servant-people/

p. 59   On Humor: zelenskiy_official, Instagram, April 1, 2017.
         https://www.instagram.com/p/BSVOnVagB-S/

p. 60   On His Inauguration: Inaugural Address, May 20, 2019.
         https://www.president.gov.ua/en/news/inavguracijna
         -promova-prezidenta-ukrayini-volodimira-zelensk
         -55489

p. 61   On Independence: Speech, August 24, 2019. https://www
         .president.gov.ua/en/news/vistup-prezidenta-ukrayini-pid
         -chas-urochistostej-z-nagodi-d-56937

p. 61   On Independence: Speech August 24, 2020. https://www
         .president.gov.ua/en/news/promova-prezidenta-z-nagodi
         -dnya-nezalezhnosti-ukrayini-62953

p. 62   On Israel: David Horovitz, "A Serious Man." *Times of
         Israel*, January 19, 2020. https://www.timesofisrael.com
         /a-serious-man-zelensky-bids-to-address-ukraines-dark
         -past-brighten-its-future/

p. 62   On Israel: "Ukraine President Zelensky's Speech to Israeli
         lawmakers." *Times of Israel*, March 20, 2022. https://www
         .timesofisrael.com/full-text-ukraine-president-zelenskys
         -speech-to-israeli-lawmakers/

p. 63   On Japanese Culture: zelenskiy_official, Instagram,
         October 22, 2019. https://www.instagram.com/p/B36w
         YDCFnf_/

p. 64   On Being Jewish: "Interview Vladimir Zelensky: 'As Soon
         As I Plan on Going into Politics, I'll Tell You.'" *Pavel
         Maljutin*, March 11, 2018. https://www.youtube.com
         /watch?v=1tcBoqj2yEI

p. 64   On Being Jewish: David Horovitz, "A Serious Man."
         Times of Israel, January 19, 2020. https://www.times
         ofisrael.com/a-serious-man-zelensky-bids-to-address
         -ukraines-dark-past-brighten-its-future/

p. 64   On Being Jewish: Andrew Higgins, "Ukraine's Newly
         Elected President Is Jewish. So Is Its Prime Minister.
         Not All Jews There Are Pleased." *The New York Times*,
         April 24, 2019. https://www.nytimes.com/2019/04/24
         /world/europe/volodomyr-zelensky-ukraine-jewish
         -president.html

p. 64   On Being Jewish: "Historical STAND-UP by President
         Zelensky!" *The Vesti*, March 27, 2019. https://www
         .youtube.com/watch?v=113lSKRvjGM&t=130s

p. 65   On Journalists: "Thanks everyone!" *Facebook*, November
         24, 2017. https://www.facebook.com/zelenskiy.official
         /videos/1939102139673486/?t=0

p. 66   On Keeping Busy: "Behind the Eyes of Vladimir
         Zelensky." *Behind Their Eyes*, 2010. https://www.youtube
         .com/watch?v=1W2fTpGNIFY

p. 66   On Keeping Busy: "Vladimir Zelensky Spoke About Life
         with his Wife and Grown-up Son." *Viva*, March 15, 2016.
         https://viva.ua/lifestar/interesting-conversation/36100
         -vladimir-zelenskiy-rasskazal-o-jizni-s-suprugoy-i
         -povzroslevshem-sine.html

p. 67   On His Law Degree: "Interview Vladimir Zelensky:
         'As Soon As I Plan on Going into Politics, I'll Tell You.'"
         Pavel Maljutin, March 11, 2018. https://www.youtube
         .com/watch?v=1tcBoqj2yEI

p. 68   On Leadership: Speech to the United Nations, September 25,
         2019. https://www.president.gov.ua/en/news/vistup

-prezidenta-ukrayini-volodimira-zelenskogo-na
-zagalnih-57477

p. 68   On Leadership: "Vladimir Zelensky Spoke About Life
with his Wife and Grown-up Son." *Viva*, March 15, 2016.
https://viva.ua/lifestar/interesting-conversation/36100
-vladimir-zelenskiy-rasskazal-o-jizni-s-suprugoy-i
-povzroslevshem-sine.html

p. 69   On Leaving Ukraine for a Better Life: Christina
Khudenko, "Volodymyr Zelensky about Ukrainianness,
Laughter During the War, and Artists in Politics." *Delfi*,
July 11, 2017. https://rus.delfi.lv/showtime/news/stars
/news/krivorizhanin-vladimir-zelenskij-pro-ukrainskost
-smeh-vo-vremya-vojny-i-artistov-v-politike.d?id=49033
821&all=true

p. 69   On Leaving Ukraine for a Better Life: Interview,
Ukraine Davos The Report/Newsweek, January 20, 2020.
http://ukrainedavos.the-report.com/interview/h-e
-volodymyr-zelensky/

p. 70   On Legalizing Medical Marijuana: Vladislav Krasinsky,
Sergey Shcerbina, "Volodymyr Zelensky: It Is Beneficial for
Us to Dissolve the Rada." *RBC-Ukraine*, April 18, 2019.
https://www.rbc.ua/rus/news/vladimir-zelenskiy-nam
-vygodno-raspustit-1555546435.html

p. 71   On Legalizing Prostitution: Vladislav Krasinsky, Sergey
Shcerbina, "Volodymyr Zelensky: It Is Beneficial for Us to
Dissolve the Rada." *RBC-Ukraine*, April 18, 2019. https
://www.rbc.ua/rus/news/vladimir-zelenskiy-nam-vygodno
-raspustit-1555546435.html

p. 72   On LGBTQ Rights: Press conference, October 10, 2019.
https://twitter.com/Hromadske/status/1183378101788540928

p. 73   On the Limits of Social Media: zelenskiy_official,
Instagram, June 20, 2021. https://www.instagram.com
/p/CQV5aedhxe3/

p. 74   On Love: "Volodymyr Zelensky: 'For Modern People, Love
is Just Sex.'" *Viva*, January 16, 2014. https://viva.ua/lifestar
/interesting-conversation/25144-vladimir-zelenskiy-dlya
-sovremennih-lyudey-lyubovj-eto-prosto-seks.html

p. 75   On Making It As An Actor: "Behind the Eyes of Vladimir Zelensky." *Behind Their Eyes*, 2010. https://www.youtube.com/watch?v=1W2fTpGNIFY

p. 76   On Making Mistakes: Speech, April 10, 2020. https://www.president.gov.ua/en/news/zmini-do-byudzhetu-pokarannya-za-vipalyuvannya-travi-ta-pidt-60581

p. 76   On Making Mistakes: "Poroshenko Still Thinks He's President." BBC, October 12, 2020. https://www.youtube.com/watch?v=Bc0G0Y7Rubc

p. 77   On Manners: "Behind the Eyes of Vladimir Zelensky." *Behind Their Eyes*, 2010. https://www.youtube.com/watch?v=1W2fTpGNIFY

p. 78   On His Marriage: Dmitry Gordon, "Zelensky: If I Am Elected President, First They Will Sling Mud at Me, Then They Will Respect Me, and Then They Will Cry When I Leave." *GordonUA.com*, December 26, 2018. https://gordonua.com/publications/zelenskiy-esli-menya-vyberut-prezidentom-snachala-budut-oblivat-gryazyu-zatem-uvazhat-a-potom-plakat-kogda-uydu-609294.html

p. 78   On His Marriage: zelenskiy_official, *Instagram*, February 6, 2020. https://www.instagram.com/p/B8NxhkTlByV/

p. 78   On His Marriage: Olga Kungurtseva & Vsevolod Tsymbal, "Kaveenshchik and TV Presenter Vladimir Zelensky: There Are No Friends in KVN." *Gordon Boulevard*, May 15, 2006. http://bulvar.com.ua/gazeta/archive/s20_3722/2225.html

p. 78   On His Marriage: "Volodymyr Zelenskyi Talked About His Kiss with Vira Brezhnev," *Social Life*, February 26, 2016. https://www.youtube.com/watch?v=6xqymY9MEtQ

p. 79   On His Marriage: "Volodymyr Zelenskyi Talked About His Kiss with Vira Brezhnev." *Social Life*, February 26, 2016. https://www.youtube.com/watch?v=6xqymY9MEtQ

p. 80   On the Military: Inaugural Address, May 20, 2019. https://www.president.gov.ua/en/news/inavguracijna-promova-prezidenta-ukrayini-volodimira-zelensk-55489

p. 80   On the Military: Speech, October 20, 2020. https://www.president.gov.ua/en/news/poslannya-prezidenta-ukrayini-volodimira-zelenskogo-do-verho-64717

p. 80   On the Military: Speech, October 20, 2020. https://www
         .president.gov.ua/en/news/poslannya-prezidenta-ukrayini
         -volodimira-zelenskogo-do-verho-64717

p. 80   On the Military: *Breakfast with 1+1*, August 21, 2014.
         https://www.youtube.com/watch?v=dR2PuC4anA8

p. 81   On the Military: Bryan Alexander, "Ukrainian President
         Zelensky Addresses Grammys." *USA Today*, April 3,
         2022. https://www.usatoday.com/story/entertainment
         /music/2022/04/03/ukrainian-president-zelensky
         -addresses-grammy-awards/7265764001/

p. 82   On His Mission: Inaugural Address, May 20, 2019.
         https://www.president.gov.ua/en/news/inavguracijna
         -promova-prezidenta-ukrayini-volodimira-zelensk-55489

p. 83   On National Autonomy: Speech, March 12, 2021. https
         ://www.president.gov.ua/en/news/zvernennya-prezidenta
         -ukrayini-shodo-ostannih-rishen-rnbo-67109

p. 84   On NATO: "Zelensky: 'I Have a Simple Question for
         Biden—Why Is Ukraine Still Not Part of NATO?'"
         Finbalance, February 1, 2021. https://finbalance.com.ua
         /news/zelenskiy-v-mene--proste-pitannya-do-baydena
         ---chomu-ukrana-dosi-ne-v-nato

p. 84   On NATO: "Poroshenko Still Thinks He's President."
         BBC, October 12, 2020. https://www.youtube.com
         /watch?v=Bc0G0Y7Rubc

p. 84   On NATO: "Poroshenko Still Thinks He's President."
         BBC, October 12, 2020. https://www.youtube.com
         /watch?v=Bc0G0Y7Rubc

p. 85   On NATO: David Muir, ABC News, March 8, 2022.
         https://abcnews.go.com/Politics/Zelensky-challenges
         -us-limits-ukraine-note/story?id=83302732

p. 85   On NATO: "VIP with Natalia Moseichuk: Volodymyr
         Zelensky." *Telechannel 1+1*, June 24, 2021. https://youtube
         /FixCRg1mNpg

p. 86   On Partnering with Other Nations: Speech, February 19,
         2022. https://www.president.gov.ua/en/news/vistup
         -prezidenta-ukrayini-na-58-j-myunhenskij-konferenciyi
         -72997

p. 87   On Patience: "Vladimir Zelensky Spoke about Life with his
         Wife and Grown-up Son." *Viva*, March 15, 2016. https://viva
         .ua/lifestar/interesting-conversation/36100-vladimir-zelenskiy
         -rasskazal-o-jizni-s-suprugoy-i-povzroslevshem-sine.html
p. 88   On Paying Him Respect: "Hottest Quotes of Zelensky as
         President." NASH 20.05, May 20, 2020. https://www
         .youtube.com/watch?v=DJJzC9Pp1PE
p. 89   On Peace: "Poroshenko Still Thinks He's President."
         BBC, October 12, 2020. https://www.youtube.com
         /watch?v=Bc0G0Y7Rubc
p. 89   On Peace: Simon Shuster, "I Don't Trust Anyone at All."
         Time, December 2, 2019. https://time.com/5742108
         /ukraine-zelensky-interview-trump-putin-europe/
p. 89   On Peace: Speech, February 19, 2022. https://www
         .president.gov.ua/en/news/vistup-prezidenta-ukrayini-na
         -58-j-myunhenskij-konferenciyi-72997
p. 89   On Peace: David Horovitz, "A Serious Man." *The Times of
         Israel*, January 19, 2020. https://www.timesofisrael.com/a
         -serious-man-zelensky-bids-to-address-ukraines-dark
         -past-brighten-its-future/
p. 90   On People: Viv Groskop, "How Funny Is the Comedian
         Who May Be Ukraine's Next President?" *The Guardian*,
         April 2, 2019. https://www.theguardian.com/stage
         /shortcuts/2019/apr/02/volodymyr-zelenskiy-how-funny
         -comedian-ukraine-president
p. 91   On Performing: "Behind the Eyes of Vladimir Zelensky."
         Behind Their Eyes, 2010. https://www.youtube.com
         /watch?v=1W2fTpGNIFY
p. 91   On Performing: "Behind the Eyes of Vladimir Zelensky."
         Behind Their Eyes, 2010. https://www.youtube.com
         /watch?v=1W2fTpGNIFY
p. 91   On Performing: *Breakfast with 1+1*, August 21, 2014.
         https://www.youtube.com/watch?v=dR2PuC4anA8
p. 91   On Performing: "Interview Vladimir Zelensky: 'As Soon
         As I Plan on Going into Politics, I'll Tell You.'" *Pavel
         Maljutin*, March 11, 2018. https://www.youtube.com
         /watch?v=1tcBoqj2yEI

p. 92   On His Personal Philosophy: "Vladimir Zelensky: 'Alena
         Shoptenko and I Love Each Other . . . Only on the
         Floor.'" *Facts.ua*, November 24, 2006. https://culture
         .fakty.ua/51044-vladimir-zelenskij-quot-my-s-alenoj
         -shoptenko-lyubim-drug-druga-tolko-na-parkete-quot
p. 92   On His Personal Philosophy: Stephen Mulvey, "Ukraine's
         Volodymyr Zelensky: The Comedian President Who is
         Rising to the Moment." BBC News, February 26, 2022.
         https://www.bbc.com/news/world-europe-59667938
p. 92   On His Personal Philosophy: Speech, October 20, 2020.
         https://www.president.gov.ua/en/news/poslannya-prezidenta
         -ukrayini-volodimira-zelenskogo-do-verho-64717
p. 92   On His Personal Philosophy: "Zelensky Vladimir."
         Liga.net, June 5, 2018. https://web.archive.org
         /web/20190102050545/https://file.liga.net/persons
         /vladimir-zelenskii
p. 92   On His Personal Philosophy: zelenskiy_official, Instagram,
         August 7, 2017. https://www.instagram.com/p/BXfDv09
         AVUI/
p. 93   On His Personal Philosophy: "Volodymyr Zelensky In
         His Own Words." *The Economist*, March 27, 2022. https
         ://www.economist.com/europe/2022/03/27/volodymyr
         -zelensky-in-his-own-words
p. 94   On His Personal Wealth: Dmitry Gordon, "Zelensky:
         If I Am Elected President, First They Will Sling Mud
         at Me, Then They Will Respect Me, and Then They
         Will Cry When I Leave." *GordonUA.com* December 26,
         2018. https://gordonua.com/publications/zelenskiy-esli
         -menya-vyberut-prezidentom-snachala-budut-oblivat
         -gryazyu-zatem-uvazhat-a-potom-plakat-kogda-uydu
         -609294.html
p. 95   On Playing a President on TV vs. Real Life: Shaun
         Walker & Andrew Roth, "Volodymyr Zelensky: 'My
         White House Invitation? I Was Told It's Being Prepared.'"
         The Guardian, March 7, 2020. https://www.theguardian.
         com/world/2020/mar/07/volodymyr-zelenskiy-tv-comic
         -who-became-ukraine-president-trump-putin

p. 96   On the Police: "Behind the Eyes of Vladimir Zelensky."
          Behind Their Eyes, 2010. https://www.youtube.com/watch
          ?v=1W2fTpGNIFY
p. 97   On Politics: Joshua Yaffa, "Ukraine's Unlikely President,
          Promising a New Style of Politics, Gets a Taste of Trump's
          Swamp." *The New Yorker*, November 4, 2019. https://www
          .newyorker.com/magazine/2019/11/04/how-trumps
          -emissaries-put-pressure-on-ukraines-new-president
p. 97   On Politics: Olena Roschenko, "Zelensky Responded
          to the 'Cat in the Bag' and Talked about the Strategy."
          Ukraine Pravda, April 18, 2019. https://www.pravda.com
          .ua/news/2019/04/18/7212668/
p. 97   On Politics: Vladislav Krasinsky and Sergey Shcherbina,
          "Volodymyr Zelensky: It Is Beneficial for Us to Dissolve
          the Rada." *RBC-Ukraine*, April 18, 2019. https://www
          .rbc.ua/rus/news/vladimir-zelenskiy-nam-vygodno
          -raspustit-1555546435.html
p. 98   On His Popularity: Anton Troianovski, "'Parallel
          Universe': The Front-Runner Seeking to be Ukraine's
          President Plays One on TV." *The Washington Post*, March 9,
          2019. https://www.washingtonpost.com/world/europe
          /parallel-universe-the-front-runner-seeking-to-be
          -ukraines-president-plays-one-on-tv/2019/03/09/2a4cc22e
          -3a8c-11e9-b10b-f05a22e75865_story.html
p. 98   On His Popularity: Matthew Chance, "Zelensky Urges
          Biden To Send Strong Message on Russia." CNN, March 1,
          2022. https://www.cnn.com/2022/03/01/europe/volodymyr
          -zelensky-ukraine-cnn-interview-intl/index.html
p. 99   On Post-Soviet Life: Joshua Yaffa, "Ukraine's Unlikely
          President, Promising a New Style of Politics, Gets a Taste
          of Trump's Swamp." *The New Yorker*, November 4, 2019.
          https://www.newyorker.com/magazine/2019/11/04
          /how-trumpsemissaries-put-pressure-on-ukraines-new
          -president
p. 100   On His Predecessor, Petro Poroshenko: "Top 10 Best
          Moments with Zelensky." *Last Chance*, September 29,
          2019. https://www.youtube.com/watch?v=eVop1d05FsI

p. 100   On His Predecessor, Petro Poroshenko: "Top 10 Best Moments with Zelensky." *Last Chance*, September 29, 2019. https://www.youtube.com/watch?v=eVop1d05FsI

p. 101   On Being President: Mark MacKinnon, "Ukrainian President Praises Relationship with Trudeau." *The Globe and Mail*, June 21, 2020. https://www.theglobeandmail .com/world/article-ukrainian-president-praises -relationship-with-trudeau-but-mum-on/

p. 101   On Being President: Interview, *Ukraine Davos The Report /Newsweek*, January 20, 2020. http://ukrainedavos.the -report.com/interview/h-e-volodymyr-zelensky/

p. 101   On Being President: Inaugural address, May 20, 2019. https://www.president.gov.ua/en/news/inavguracija -promova-prezidenta-ukrayini-volodimira-zelensk -55489

p. 101   On Being President: "Volodymyr Zelensky in His Own Words." *The Economist*, March 27, 2022. https://www .economist.com/europe/2022/03/27/volodymyr-zelensky -in-his-own-words

p. 102   On Being President: Speech, October 13, 2019. https ://www.president.gov.ua/en/news/prezident-u-zvernenni -do-gromadyan-ya-prisyagnuv-boroniti-su-57789

p. 102   On Being President: Shaun Walker & Andrew Roth, "Volodymyr Zelensky: 'My White House Invitation? I Was Told It's Being Prepared." *The Guardian*, March 7, 2020. https://www.theguardian.com/world/2020/mar/07 /volodymyr-zelenskiy-tv-comic-who-became-ukraine -president-trump-putin

p. 102   On Being President: "Interview with the President." *TSN*, November 7, 2019. https://www.youtube.com/watch?v =5O1TSVyf7ig

p. 103   On President Biden: Speech, April 2, 2021. https://www .president.gov.ua/en/news/zvernennya-prezidenta-volo dimira-zelenskogo-shodo-rishen-rnb-67761

p. 103   On President Biden: Libby Cathey, "Ukraine's Zelenskyy invokes Pearl Harbor, 9/11, calls out Biden in plea to Congress for more US help", ABC News, March 16, 2022,

https://abcnews.go.com/Politics/ukraines-zelenskyy
-invokes-pearl-harbor-911-calls-biden/story?id=83458095

p. 103   On President Biden: David Lawler, Zelensky Interview
Transcript. *Axios*, June 6, 2021. https://www.document
cloud.org/documents/20798133-zelensky-interview
-transcript

p. 104   On President Trump: "Zelensky: 'I Have a Simple
Question for Biden—Why is Ukraine Still Not Part of
NATO?'" *Finbalance*, February 1, 2021. https://finbalance
.com.ua/news/zelenskiy-v-mene--proste-pitannya-do
-baydena---chomu-ukrana-dosi-ne-v-nato

p. 104   On President Trump: Georgi Kantchev and Ann
M. Simmons, "Ukraine's Zelensky Finds Battling
Corruption Is Harder in Real Life Than It Was on TV."
The Wall Street Journal, May 18, 2020. https://www.wsj
.com/articles/ukraines-zelensksy-finds-battling
-corruption-is-harder-in-real-life-than-it-was-on-tv
-11589792725

p. 104   On President Trump: "Zelensky: 'I Have a Simple
Question for Biden—Why is Ukraine Still Not Part of
NATO?'" *Finbalance*, February 1, 2021. https://finbalance
.com.ua/news/zelenskiy-v-mene--proste-pitannya-do
-baydena---chomu-ukrana-dosi-ne-v-nato

p. 105   On President Trump: David Horovitz, "A Serious Man."
The Times of Israel, January 19, 2020. https://www.times
ofisrael.com/a-serious-man-zelensky-bids-to-address
-ukraines-dark-past-brighten-its-future/

p. 105   On President Trump: Simon Shuster, "I Don't Trust
Anyone at All." *Time*, December 2, 2019. https://time
.com/5742108/ukraine-zelensky-interview-trump-putin
-europe/

p. 105   On President Trump: Joshua Yaffa, "Ukraine's Unlikely
President, Promising a New Style of Politics, Gets a Taste
of Trump's Swamp." *The New Yorker*, November 4, 2019.
https://www.newyorker.com/magazine/2019/11/04
/how-trumps-emissaries-put-pressure-on-ukraines-new
-president

p. 106   On His Presidential Office: Shaun Walker & Andrew
          Roth, "Volodymyr Zelensky: 'My White House
          Invitation? I Was Told It's Being Prepared." *The Guardian*,
          March 7, 2020. https://www.theguardian.com
          /world/2020/mar/07/volodymyr-zelenskiy-tv-comic-who
          -became-ukraine-president-trump-putin

p. 106   On His Presidential Office: Joshua Yaffa, "Ukraine's
          Unlikely President, Promising a New Style of Politics,
          Gets a Taste of Trump's Swamp." *The New Yorker*,
          November 4, 2019. https://www.newyorker.com
          /magazine/2019/11/04/how-trumps-emissaries-put
          -pressure-on-ukraines-new-president

p. 107   On Prosecuting Oligarchs: "Interview with Vladimir
          Zelensky," *Ze!President*, March 21, 2019. https://www
          .youtube.com/watch?v=Ls0tv5M6fMs

p. 108   On Putin: "Volodymyr Zelensky In His Own Words."
          The Economist, March 27, 2022. https://www.economist.com
          /europe/2022/03/27/volodymyr-zelensky-in-his-own-words

p. 108   On Putin: Bernard-Henri Lévy, "Ukraine's Hero
          President Z." *Tablet*, February 28, 2022. https://www
          .tabletmag.com/sections/israel-middle-east/articles
          /ukraines-hero-president-z

p. 108   On Putin: "Zelenskyi's Monologue—Kiev, Mother of
          Russian Cities. Evening Kvartal from April 12, 2014."
          Studio Kvartal 95 Online, April 13, 2014. https://www
          .youtube.com/watch?v=0KkSP9N27w8

p. 109   On Putin: Bernard-Henri Lévy, "The Comedian vs. The
          Hero of Ukraine." *The Wall Street Journal*, April 8, 2019.
          https://www.wsj.com/articles/the-comedian-vs-the-hero
          -of-ukraine-11554761154

p. 110   On Religion: Vladislav Krasinsky and Sergey Shcherbina,
          "Volodymyr Zelensky: It Is Beneficial for Us to Dissolve
          the Rada." *RBC-Ukraine*, April 18, 2019. https://www
          .rbc.ua/rus/news/vladimir-zelenskiy-nam-vygodno
          -raspustit-1555546435.html

p. 110   On Religion: David Horovitz, "A Serious Man." *The Times
          of Israel*, January 19, 2020. https://www.timesofisrael

.com/a-serious-man-zelensky-bids-to address-ukraines
-dark-past-brighten-its-future/

p. 110   On Religion: Dmitry Gordon, "Zelensky: If I Am Elected
President, First They Will Sling Mud at Me, Then They
Will Respect Me, and Then They Will Cry When I
Leave." *GordonUA.com,* December 26, 2018. https
://gordonua.com/publications/zelenskiy-esli-menya
-vyberut-prezidentom-snachala-budut oblivat-gryazyu
-zatem-uvazhat-a-potom-plakat-kogda-uydu-609294.html

p. 110   On Religion: "Authorities Should Not Interfere in Church
Affairs." *Interfax,* August 8, 2019. https://ua.interfax.com
.ua/news/political/606251.html

p. 111   On Relying on International Financial Aid: "Zelensky
Compared Ukraine to 'An Actress In A German Adult
Film.'" *GordonUA.com,* September 11, 2016. https://gordon
ua.com/news/politics/zelenskiy-na-festivale-v-yurmale
-sravnil-ukrainu-s-aktrisoy-nemeckogo-filma-dlya
-vzroslyh-gotovoy-prinyat-v-lyubom-kolichestve-s-lyuboy
-storony-149665.html

p. 111   On Relying on International Financial Aid: "Zelensky
Compared Ukraine to 'An Actress In A German Adult
Film.'" *GordonUA.com,* September 11, 2016. https://gordon
ua.com/news/politics/zelenskiy-na-festivale-v-yurmale
-sravnil-ukrainu-s-aktrisoy-nemeckogo filma-dlya
-vzroslyh-gotovoy-prinyat-v-lyubom-kolichestve-s-lyuboy
-storony-149665.html

p. 112   On Remembering the Holocaust: David Horovitz,
"A Serious Man." *The Times of Israel,* January 19,
2020. https://www.timesofisrael.com/a-serious-man
-zelensky-bids-to-address-ukraines-dark-past-brighten
-its-future/

p. 112   On Remembering the Holocaust: Speech, May 9, 2021.
https://www.president.gov.ua/en/news/zvernennya-prezi
denta-ukrayini-z-nagodi-dnya-peremogi-nad-na-68341

p. 113   On Returning Donbas and Crimea: Speech, October 3,
2019. https://www.president.gov.ua/en/news/zvernennya
-prezidenta-ukrayini-volodimira-zelenskogo-57593

p. 113   On Returning Donbas and Crimea: "Zelensky With His
         Wife on TV." *ICTV*, March 24, 2019. https://web.archive
         .org/web/20190410094553/https:/www.youtube.com
         /watch?v=jzkmi1uKfQg

p. 114   On Revolution: Speech, November 21, 2020. https://www
         .president.gov.ua/en/news/zvernennya-prezidenta-ukrayini
         -z-nagodi-dnya-gidnosti-ta-svo-65169

p. 115   On Romance: "Volodymyr Zelensky: 'For Modern People,
         Love is Just Sex.'" *Viva*, January 16, 2014. https://viva.ua
         /lifestar/interesting-conversation/25144-vladimir
         -zelenskiy-dlya-sovremennih-lyudey-lyubovj-eto-prosto
         -seks.html

p. 116   On Running for President: Dmitry Gordon, "Zelensky:
         If I Am Elected President, First They Will Sling Mud at
         Me, Then They Will Respect Me, and Then They Will
         Cry When I Leave." *GordonUA.com*, December 26, 2018.
         https://gordonua.com/publications/zelenskiy-esli-menya
         -vyberut-prezidentom-snachala-budut-oblivat-gryazyu
         -zatem-uvazhat-a-potom-plakat-kogda-uydu-609294.html

p. 116   On Running for President: Georgi Kantchev, "The
         Revolution That Wasn't: Disillusioned Ukrainians Head
         to Polls." *The Wall Street Journal*, March 28, 2019. https
         ://www.wsj.com/articles/the-revolution-that-wasnt
         -disillusioned-ukrainians-head-to-polls-11553778000

p. 116   On Running for President: Olena Roschenko, "Zelensky
         Responded to the 'Cat in the Bag' and Talked About the
         Strategy." *Ukraine Pravda*, April 18, 2019. https://www
         .pravda.com.ua/news/2019/04/18/7212668/

p. 116   On Running for President: Olena Roschenko, "Zelensky
         Responded to the 'Cat in the Bag' and Talked about the
         Strategy." *Ukraine Pravda*, April 18, 2019. https://www
         .pravda.com.ua/news/2019/04/18/7212668/

p. 117   On Running for President: zelenskiy_official, Instagram,
         January 1, 2019. https://www.instagram.com/p/Bs
         GRGUalFH3/

p. 118   On Running for a Second Term: Olga Hetmanets,
         "Zelensky Answered Whether He Would Run for a

Second Term." *Ukraine Pravda*, May 20, 2021. https
://www.pravda.com.ua/news/2021/05/20/7294216/

p. 119   On Russia: David Muir, ABC News, March 8, 2022.
https://abcnews.go.com/Politics/Zelensky-challenges
-us-limits-ukraine-note/story?id=83302732

p. 119   On Russia: Interview with Vladimir Zelensky. *Ze!President*,
March 21, 2019. https://www.youtube.com/watch?v
=Ls0tv5M6fMs&t=605s

p. 119   On Russia: Stephen Mulvey, "Ukraine's Volodymyr
Zelensky: The Comedian President Who is Rising to the
Moment." BBC News, February 26, 2022. https://www
.bbc.com/news/world-europe-59667938

p. 120   On Russian Soldiers: Matthew Chance, "Zelensky Urges
Biden To Send Strong Message on Russia." CNN, March 1,
2022. https://www.cnn.com/2022/03/01/europe
/volodymyr-zelensky-ukraine-cnn-interview-intl/index.html

p. 120   On Russian Soldiers: "Volodymyr Zelensky In His Own
Words." *The Economist*, March 27, 2022. https://www
.economist.com/europe/2022/03/27/volodymyr-zelensky
-in-his-own-words

p. 120   On Russian Soldiers: zelenskiy_official, Instagram, March 3,
2022. https://www.instagram.com/p/Cb5F3emACcF/

p. 121   On Sacrifice: Interview, *Ukraine Davos The Report
/Newsweek*, January 20, 2020. http://ukrainedavos.the
-report.com/interview/h-e-volodymyr-zelensky/

p. 122   On Sanctions: "Zelensky: 'I Have a Simple Question
for Biden—Why is Ukraine Still Not Part of NATO?'"
Finbalance, February 1, 2021. https://finbalance.com.ua
/news/zelenskiy-v-mene--proste-pitannya-do-baydena
---chomu-ukrana-dosi-ne-v-nato

p. 123   On Seeing Adele Perform in Lisbon: "Star Interview:
Volodymyr Zelenskyi." *Stand Up Boys*, June 19, 2016.
https://www.youtube.com/watch?v=dkf8OK7TkLc

p. 124   On the *Servant of the People* TV Show: Dmitry Gordon,
"Zelensky: If I Am Elected President, First They Will
Sling Mud at Me, Then They Will Respect Me, and Then
They Will Cry When I Leave." *GordonUA.com*,

December 26, 2018. https://gordonua.com/publications
/zelenskiy-esli-menya-vyberut-prezidentom-snachala
-budut-oblivat-gryazyu-zatem-uvazhat-a-potom-plakat
-kogda-uydu-609294.html

p. 124   On the *Servant of the People* TV Show: Anthony Kao,
"Interview: Vladimir Zelenskiy on Playing Ukraine's
President in *Servant of the People*." *Cinema Escapist*,
August 22, 2017. https://www.cinemaescapist.com
/2017/08/interview-vladimir-zelenskiy-playing
-ukraines-president-servant-people/

p. 125   On Speaking English: "Vladimir Zelensky: Permanent
Leader of the Kvartal 95 Studio." *ILand TV*, April 19, 2017.
https://www.youtube.com/watch?v=pMiJ17GDCz0

p. 125   On Speaking English: "*Volodymyr Zelensky on Breakfast
with 1+1.*" March 7, 2013. https://www.youtube.com
/watch?v=fnS_RPhG7Vc

p. 126   On Speaking Russian vs. Ukrainian: "Ukrainian Family
Through the Eyes of Russians." *Evening Kvartal*, March 10,
2017. https://www.youtube.com/watch?v=8hj0Gic5irg

p. 126   On Speaking Russian vs. Ukrainian: "Zelensky: You Need
to Let People in Donetsk Speak Whatever Language They
Want." *Donetsk News*, July 8, 2019. https://dnews.dn.ua
/news/720982

p. 126   On Speaking Russian vs. Ukrainian: "Vladimir Zelensky:
Permanent Leader of the Kvartal 95 Studio." *ILand TV*,
April 19, 2017. https://www.youtube.com/watch?v
=pMiJ17GDCz0

p. 126   On Speaking Russian vs. Ukrainian: "Volodymyr Zelenskyi
Learned Ukrainian with a Private Tutor." *Social Life*, April 15,
2017. https://www.youtube.com/watch?v=bor3ywG6drw

p. 127   On Speaking Russian vs. Ukrainian: Interview with
Vladimir Zelensky. *Ze!President*, March 21, 2019. https
://www.youtube.com/watch?v=Ls0tv5M6fMs&t=605s

p. 127   On Speaking Russian vs. Ukrainian: Oleksiy Matsuka,
"Who Are You? An Interview with President Volodymyr
Zelensky on Donbas and Crimea." *House TV*, August 5,
2021. https://kanaldom.tv/uk/kto-ty-sam-dlya-sebya

-otvet-intervyu-prezidenta-vladimira-zelenskogo-o
-donbasse-i-kryme/

p. 127   On Speaking Russian vs. Ukrainian: Dmytryi
Ponomarenko, "After 25 Years of Work as a Russian
Language Comic Zelensky Said That Jokes in Ukrainian
Are the Funniest." *Ukrainian News,* November 9, 2021.
https://ukranews.com/ua/news/813221-pislya-25-rokiv
-roboty-rosijskomovnym-komikom-zelenskyj-zayavyv
-shho-anekdoty-ukrayinskoyu

p. 128   On Swimming: zelenskiy_official, Instagram, April 9,
2019. https://www.instagram.com/p/BwBvmZtl8XS/

p. 129   On Technological Innovation: Speech, October 20, 2020.
https://www.president.gov.ua/en/news/poslannya-prezidenta
-ukrayini-volodimira-zelenskogo-do-verho-64717

p. 129   On Technological Innovation: "In California, Zelensky Meets
with Ukrainians Working at Silicon Valley Companies."
UKRInform.com, September 4, 2021. https://web.archive.org
/web/20210906222855/https://www.ukrinform.net/rubric
-economy/3309992-in-california-zelensky-meets-with
-ukrainians-working-at-silicon-valley-companies.html

p. 129   On Technological Innovation: "Zelensky: We Have a Lot
of Fuckups." *iForum 2019,* May 23, 2019. https://www.you
tube.com/watch?v=iB0UkcpXRws

p. 130   On Traveling Into Space: MS Rybik, "Interview: Vera
Brezhneva and Vladimir Zelensky." *Elle Ukraine,* March 2,
2016. https://elle.ua/ludi/interview/intervyu-vera-brejneva
-i-vladimir-zelenskiy/

p. 131   On Trolls: zelenskiy_official, Instagram, January 28, 2019.
https://www.instagram.com/p/BtK62OMBnqc/

p. 131   On Trolls: "Zelensky: Me, a Clown? No Problem."
At Gordon's, March 23, 2019. https://www.youtube.com
/watch?v=I5yKqKsXWbc

p. 132   On Trust: Simon Shuster, "I Don't Trust Anyone at All."
Time, December 2, 2019. https://time.com/5742108
/ukraine-zelensky-interview-trump-putin-europe/

p. 132   On Trust: "They Steal with a Smile!" *Ze!President,* July 17,
2019. https://www.youtube.com/watch?v=hKJ7gOZ70CU

p. 133   On Truth: Speech, March 4, 2020. https://www
         .president.gov.ua/en/news/vistup-prezidenta-ukrayini
         -volodimira-zelenskogo-na-pozacher-60017
p. 134   On Ukraine: Speech, August 24, 2021. https://www
         .president.gov.ua/en/news/promova-prezidenta
         -volodimira-zelenskogo-z-nagodi-30-yi-rich-70333
p. 134   On Ukraine: Speech, August 24, 2019. https://www
         .president.gov.ua/en/news/vistup-prezidenta-ukrayini-pid
         -chas-urochistostej-z-nagodi-d-56937
p. 134   On Ukraine: Jonathan Swan, "Exclusive: Ukraine's
         Zelensky Calls Riots 'Strong Blow' to U.S. Democracy.'"
         Axios on HBO, January 31, 2021. https://www.axios.com
         /ukraine-zelensky-capitol-riots-axios-hbo-f223c6d4-1aee
         -4779-a26d-f5f0eefb90f2.html
p. 134   On Ukraine: Matthew Chance, "Zelensky Urges Biden to
         Send Strong Message on Russia." CNN, March 1, 2022.
         https://www.cnn.com/2022/03/01/europe/volodymyr
         -zelensky-ukraine-cnn-interview-intl/index.html
p. 135   On Ukraine's History with Russia: Olga Korelina, "More
         like Cain and Abel." *Meduza*, July 31, 2021. https://meduza
         .io/en/feature/2021/07/13/more-like-cain-and-abel
p. 135   On Ukraine's History with Russia: Kvitka Perehinets,
         "Zelensky at Stanford: 'Russia's Policy Is to Take, Not
         Give.'" *Kyiv Post*, September 3, 2021. https://www.kyiv
         post.com/ukraine-politics/zelensky-at-stanford-russias
         -policy-is-to-take-not-give.html
p. 136   On Ukrainian Autonomy: Joshua Yaffa, "Ukraine's Unlikely
         President, Promising a New Style of Politics, Gets a Taste of
         Trump's Swamp." *The New Yorker*, November 4, 2019. https
         ://www.newyorker.com/magazine/2019/11/04/how-trumps
         -emissaries-put-pressure-on-ukraines-new-president
p. 137   On Ukrainian Sacrifice: David Lawler, Zelensky Interview
         Transcript. *Axios*, June 6, 2021. https://www.documentcloud
         .org/documents/20798133-zelensky-interview-transcript
p. 138   On Ukrainian Spirit: Speech, November 21, 2021. https
         ://www.president.gov.ua/en/news/zvernennya-prezidenta
         -ukrayini-z-nagodi-dnya-gidnosti-ta-svo-71637

p. 138   On Ukrainian Spirit: Melissa Morgan, "'Everything
          is Possible in Ukraine': President Volodymyr Zelensky
          Addresses Stanford Community During Historic Visit."
          Stanford.edu, September 9, 2021. https://fsi.stanford.edu
          /news/%E2%80%98everything-possible-ukraine%E
          2%80%99-president-volodymyr-zelensky-addresses
          -stanford-community-during

p. 138   On Ukrainian Spirit: Cameron Jenkins, "Interpreter
          Breaks Down During Zelensky's Remarks about
          Children's Deaths." *The Hill*, March 1, 2022. https
          ://thehill.com/policy/international/europe/596247
          -interpreter-breaks-down-during-zelenskys-remarks
          -about

p. 138   On Ukrainian Spirit: Oliver Pieper, "Ukraine's Volodymyr
          Zelensky: From Comedian to National Hero." *Deutsche
          Welle*, February 26, 2022. https://www.dw.com/en
          /ukraines-volodymyr-Zelensky-from-comedian-to
          -national-hero/a-60924507

p. 138   On Ukrainian Spirit: Speech, March 12, 2021. https
          ://www.president.gov.ua/en/news/zvernennya-prezidenta
          -ukrayini-shodo-ostannih-rishen-rnbo-67109

p. 139   On Ukrainian Spirit: Zachary Basu, "Zelensky: 'We Are
          a Nation That Broke the Enemy's Plans in a Week.'" *Axios*,
          March 3, 2022. https://www.axios.com/zelensky
          -video-address-russia-invasion-019310e6-a3f7-48b5-af2f
          -46be88fb2966.html

p. 139   On Ukrainian Spirit: Zachary Basu, "Zelensky Addresses
          European Parliament: 'No One Is Going to Break Us.'"
          Axios, March 1, 2022. https://www.axios.com/zelensky
          -video-european-parliament-address-ukraine-ed88a2e1
          -ff9e-471c-9a4d-92e0406ff541.html

p. 140   On Ukrainians Living in Russian Occupied Territories:
          Oleksiy Matsuka, "Who Are You? An Interview with
          President Volodymyr Zelensky on Donbas and Crimea."
          House TV, August 5, 2021. https://kanaldom.tv/uk/kto
          -ty-sam-dlya-sebya-otvet-intervyu-prezidenta-vladimira
          -zelenskogo-o-donbasse-i-kryme/

187

p. 140　On Ukrainians Living in Russian Occupied Territories: Oleksiy Matsuka, "An Interview with President Volodymyr Zelensky on Donbas and Crimea." *House TV*, August 5, 2021. https://kanaldom.tv/uk/kto-ty-sam-dlya-sebya-otvet-intervyu -prezidenta-vladimira-zelenskogo-o-donbasse-i-kryme/

p. 141　On the United Nations: Speech to the United Nations, September 23, 2021. https://www.president.gov.ua/en /news/vistup-prezidenta-ukrayini-volodimira-zelenskogo -na-zagalnih-70773

p. 141　On the United Nations: Speech to the United Nations, September 23, 2020. https://www.president.gov.ua/en /news/vistup-prezidenta-ukrayini-volodimira-zelenskogo -na-zagalnih-63889

p. 142　On the United States: Interview, *Ukraine Davos The Report/ Newsweek*, January 20, 2020. http://ukrainedavos.the -report.com/interview/h-e-volodymyr-zelensky/

p. 142　On the United States: "Best Quotes of Zelensky from the Press Marathon." *Current Time*, October 11, 2019. https ://www.currenttime.tv/a/zelenskiy/30211371.html

p. 143　On Victory: Simon Shuster, "I Don't Trust Anyone at All." *Time*, December 2, 2019. https://time.com/5742108 /ukraine-zelensky-interview-trump-putin-europe/

p. 143　On Victory: "Volodymyr Zelensky in His Own Words." *The Economist*, March 27, 2022. https://www.economist .com/europe/2022/03/27/volodymyr-zelensky-in-his -own-words

p. 143　On Victory: "Volodymyr Zelensky in His Own Words." *The Economist*, March 27, 2022. https://www.economist .com/europe/2022/03/27/volodymyr-zelensky-in-his -own-words

p. 144　On War: Dmitry Gordon, "Zelensky: If I Am Elected President, First They Will Sling Mud at Me, Then They Will Respect Me, and Then They Will Cry When I Leave." *GordonUA.com*, December 26, 2018. https ://gordonua.com/publications/zelenskiy-esli-menya -vyberut-prezidentom-snachala-budut-oblivat-gryazyu -zatem-uvazhat-a-potom-plakat-kogda-uydu-609294.html

p. 144   On War: Speech to the United Nations, September 25, 2019. https://www.president.gov.ua/en/news/vistup -prezidenta-ukrayini-volodimira-zelenskogo-na-zagalnih -57477

p. 144   On War: David Muir, ABC News, March 8, 2022. https://abcnews.go.com/Politics/Zelensky-challenges -us-limits-ukraine-note/story?id=83302732

p. 144   On War: Inaugural Address, May 20, 2019. https ://www.president.gov.ua/en/news/inavguracijna-promova -prezidenta-ukrayini-volodimira-zelensk-55489

p. 145   On War: Stephen Mulvey, "Ukraine's Volodymyr Zelensky: The Comedian President Who is Rising to the Moment." BBC News, February 26, 2022. https://www .bbc.com/news/world-europe-59667938

p. 145   On War: Fareed Zakaria, Interview With Ukraine's President Volodymyr Zelensky. CNN, March 20, 2022. https://transcripts.cnn.com/show/fzgps/date/2022-03-20 /segment/01

p. 145   On War: Speech, October 3, 2019. https://www.president .gov.ua/en/news/zvernennya-prezidenta-ukrayini-volodimira -zelenskogo-57593

p. 146   On Watching Himself on TV: Dmitry Gordon, "Zelensky: If I Am Elected President, First They Will Sling Mud at Me, Then They Will Respect Me, and Then They Will Cry When I Leave." *GordonUA.com*, December 26, 2018. https://gordonua.com/publications/zelenskiy-esli-menya -vyberut-prezidentom-snachala-budut-oblivat-gryazyu -zatem-uvazhat-a-potom-plakat-kogda-uydu-609294.html

p. 146   On Watching Himself on TV: "Behind the Eyes of Vladimir Zelensky." *Behind Their Eyes*, 2010. https://www .youtube.com/watch?v=1W2fTpGNIFY

p. 147   On His Wedding Day: "It Was a School Lineup: Volodymyr Zelensky Told About Meeting His Wife." *Today*, December 25, 2018. https://lifestyle.segodnya.ua /ua/lifestyle/showbiz/eto-byla-shkolnaya-lineyka -vladimir-zelenskiy-rasskazal-o-znakomstve-s-zhenoy -1200813.html

p. 148   On Who He Is: "Zelensky: The Servant of the People
Party is Going into Politics." *Interfax*, December 26, 2018.
https://web.archive.org/web/20190103055829/https
:/ua.interfax.com.ua/news/election2019/555634.html

p. 148   On Who He Is: "Zelensky: The Servant of the People
Party is Going into Politics." *Interfax*, December 26, 2018.
https://web.archive.org/web/20190103055829/https
:/ua.interfax.com.ua/news/election2019/555634.html

p. 148   On Who He Is: Vladislav Krasinsky and Sergey
Shcherbina, "Volodymyr Zelensky: It Is Beneficial for
Us to Dissolve the Rada." *RBC-Ukraine*, April 18, 2019.
https://www.rbc.ua/rus/news/vladimir-zelenskiy-nam
-vygodno-raspustit-1555546435.html

p. 148   On Who He Is: Kvitka Perehinets, "Zelensky at Stanford:
'Russia's Policy Is To Take, Not Give.'" *Kyiv Post*,
September 3, 2021. https://www.kyivpost.com/ukraine
-politics/zelensky-at-stanford-russias-policy-is-to-take
-not-give.html

p. 148   On Who He Is: Dmitry Gordon, "Zelensky: If I Am
Elected President, First They Will Sling Mud at Me, Then
They Will Respect Me, and Then They Will Cry When I
Leave." *GordonUA.com* December 26, 2018. https
://gordonua.com/publications/zelenskiy-esli-menya
-vyberut-prezidentom-snachala-budut-oblivat-gryazyu
-zatem-uvazhat-a-potom-plakat-kogda-uydu-609294.html

p. 148   On Who He Is: Roman Timofeev, "Ukrainians about
Ukraine: Vladimir Zelensky." *Elle Ukraine*, August 19,
2016. https://elle.ua/ludi/interview/ukraintsyi-ob-ukraine
-vladimir-zelenskiy/

p. 149   On Women: zelenskiy_official, Instagram, March 8, 2021.
https://www.instagram.com/p/CMJ09x9FJjq/

p. 149   On Women: "Putin is a Little Boy Who Can Control His
Gas: The Best Monologues of Zelensky." *Studio Kvartal 95
Online*, May 7, 2017. https://www.youtube.com/watch
?v=h_6l8Na_KNE

p. 149   On Women: "Putin is a Little Boy Who Can Control His
Gas: The Best Monologues of Zelensky." *Studio Kvartal 95*

Online, May 7, 2017. https://www.youtube.com/watch
?v=h_6l8Na_KNE

p. 150   On the Younger Generation: Speech, August 24, 2019.
           https://www.president.gov.ua/en/news/vistup-prezidenta
           -ukrayini-pid-chas-urochistostej-z-nagodi-d-56937

p. 150   On the Younger Generation: Dmitry Gordon, "Zelensky:
           If I Am Elected President, First They Will Sling Mud at
           Me, Then They Will Respect Me, and Then They Will
           Cry When I Leave." *GordonUA.com*, December 26, 2018.
           https://gordonua.com/publications/zelenskiy-esli-menya
           -vyberut-prezidentom-snachala-budut-oblivat-gryazyu
           -zatem-uvazhat-a-potom-plakat-kogda-uydu-609294.html

p. 151   On the Younger Generation: "Interview with the
           President." *TSN*, November 7, 2019. https://www.youtube
           .com/watch?v=5O1TSVyf7ig

ABOUT THE EDITORS

Lisa Rogak is the *New York Times* bestselling author of hundreds of newspaper and magazine articles, and the author of more than forty books published in over two dozen languages, including *Angry Optimist: The Life and Times of Jon Stewart, Barack Obama in His Own Words*, and *Who Is Alex Trebek?: A Biography*. www.lisarogak.com.

Daisy Gibbons is an award-winning translator from Ukrainian and Russian into English. She presently serves as a translator for the *New York Times*. Her literary translations have been published by independent publishers in the US, Canada, and Germany and have been featured in *Harper's* and *Vanity Fair*. She lived in Russia and Ukraine for several years where she worked as a translator for a Ukrainian publisher and served as publications editor for a Kyiv think tank. Gibbons attended the University of Cambridge and the State University of Nizhny Novgorod, Russia. She lives in London.